FIRST
PEOPLES
of NORTH
AMERICA

THE PEOPLE AND CULTURE OF THE

IROQUOIS

CASSIE M. LAWTON
RAYMOND BIAL

Cavendish
Square

New York

YA
974.700
LAW

Library of Congress Cataloging-in-Publication Data

Names: Lawton, Cassie M., author. | Bial, Raymond, author.
Title: The people and culture of the Iroquois / Cassie M. Lawton and Raymond Bial.
Description: New York : Cavendish Square Publishing, [2017] | Series: First peoples of North America | Includes bibliographical references and index.| Description based on print version record and CIP data provided by publisher; resource not viewed. Identifiers: LCCN 2015045725 (print) | LCCN 2015043530 (ebook) | ISBN 9781502618917 (ebook) | ISBN 9781502618900 (library bound) Subjects: LCSH: Iroquois Indians--History--Juvenile literature. | Iroquois Indians--Social life and customs--Juvenile literature. Classification: LCC E99.I7 (print) | LCC E99.I7 L39 2017 (ebook) | DDC 974.7004/9755--dc23 LC record available at http://lccn.loc.gov/2015045725

Editorial Director: David McNamara
Editor: Kristen Susienka
Copy Editor: Rebecca Rohan
Art Director: Jeffrey Talbot
Designer: Amy Greenan
Production Assistant: Karol Szymczuk
Photo Research: J8 Media

ACKNOWLEDGMENTS

This book would not have been possible without the generous help of a number of individuals and organizations that have dedicated themselves to preserving the culture of the Iroquois.

We are also very much indebted to Cavendish Square Publishing for their enthusiasm and encouragement of this series. As always, we would like to thank our families for their shining presence in our lives and their constant support on our writing journey.

CONTENTS

An Iroquois member
dresses in ceremonial
clothing.

AUTHORS' NOTE

At the dawn of the twentieth century, Native Americans were thought to be a vanishing race. However, despite four hundred years of warfare, deprivation, and disease, Native Americans have persevered. Countless thousands have lost their lives, but over the course of this century and the last, the populations of Native tribes have grown tremendously. Even as America's First Peoples struggle to adapt to modern Western life, they have also kept the flame of their traditions alive—the languages, religions, stories, and the everyday ways of life. An exhilarating renaissance in Native American culture is now sweeping the continent from coast to coast.

The First Peoples of North America books depict the social and cultural life of the major nations, from the early history of Native peoples in North America to their present-day struggles for survival and dignity. Historical and contemporary photographs of traditional subjects, as well as period illustrations, are blended throughout each book so that readers may gain a sense of family life in a tipi, a hogan, or a longhouse.

No single book can comprehensively portray the intricate and varied lifeways of an entire tribe, or nation. We only hope that young people will come away with a deeper appreciation for the rich tapestry of Native American culture—both then and now—and a keen desire to learn more about these first Americans.

A Mohawk child known as White Deer, circa 1901. The Mohawk were part of the Iroquois Confederacy.

CHAPTER ONE

When we walk upon Mother Earth, we always plant our feet carefully because we know the faces of our future generations are looking up at us from beneath the ground.

—Oren R. Lyons, Onondaga member

A CULTURE BEGINS

The story of the **Iroquois** (pronounced EAR-ah-koy in the United States and EAR-ah-kwah in Canada) begins thousands of years ago, when the first people ventured into North America by crossing a natural land bridge said to have formed on **Bering Strait**. This passage connected Asia and Alaska. Groups of people traveled over it or arrived at the continent via boat. From there, men, women, and children journeyed into what is now Canada and the

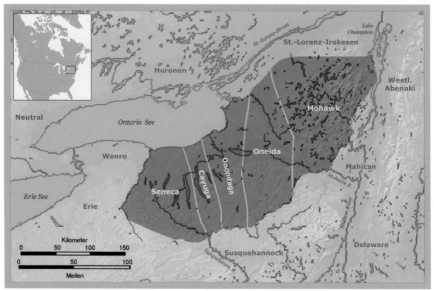

This map shows the territories of the original Five Nations of the Iroquois Confederacy.

United States. They brought with them their cultures, stories, languages, and beliefs.

Originally, people traveled in small packs, but eventually they banded into family groups to become thriving communities. Among these people were the ancestors of the Iroquois. Some of the best-known tribes of Native Americans made up the Iroquois family. Separately, they developed unique cultures at first and attacked each other regularly. Over time, however, they formed a truce and created an elite union called the **Iroquois Confederacy**, or the Iroquois League. To many other Native American groups, the Iroquois were enemies who eventually drove them from their homeland. The Iroquois, however, considered themselves established warriors and used their skills to claim their territory, marking a permanent place in the history of North America.

The Iroquois Begin

Over a thousand years ago, the tribes of the Iroquois moved into the thick green forests of what is now central New York. They settled there, built communities, and became some of the most feared tribes in the region.

The name Iroquois is a French version of **Irinakhoiw**, meaning "poisonous snakes." The name was given to them by the Ojibwa tribe, one of their rivals. Originally, the Iroquois called themselves **Haudenosaunee** (pronounced hoe-de-no-SHOW-nee), meaning "the people of the **longhouse**." However, over time, as Europeans arrived and began trading with many rival tribes, the name "Iroquois" stuck.

The Iroquois originally made their homes in the sprawling forests. The maple, elm, ash, hickory, chestnut, and beech trees blended with stands of birch trees and the eternal green of hemlock, pine, and spruce forests to the north. The forests provided food, shelter, and clothing, as well as tools, weapons, and medicine. In particular, the elm tree, which provided bark for longhouses and canoes, had special religious meaning: according to Iroquois tradition, at the center of the Earth stood the Great Elm, with huge, arching branches.

In Iroquois territory, there were no high mountains, only gentle hills from which to spot an enemy or welcome a friend. There were also many rivers and streams that formed a vast water network among the lakes. The Iroquois could easily paddle canoes throughout their territory to trade corn, beans, or animal pelts with their friends and make war on their enemies. Although trees had to be cleared to build

Many of the Iroquois tribes lived in dense forests. They believed all living things were sacred.

villages near the rivers, the land was fertile and easily worked with their stone tools. The Iroquois relied on crops of corn, beans, and squash, but they also hunted and gathered in the woods and fields.

The people of the longhouse lived within nature. The cycle of their lives revolved around four clearly defined seasons. In the spring, the sap flowed and, like delicate green lace, the buds emerged on the trees. The earth softened, warmed, and was made ready to receive seeds. In early summer, cherries and June berries, including wild strawberries and raspberries, were gathered before the long stretches of hot, dry weather. As July temperatures soared, ears of corn quickly ripened on the stalk. In the autumn, the trees provided a panorama of brilliant red, yellow, and orange foliage. Corn leaves and stalks faded to tan, pumpkins glowed orange on the damp ground, and drying beans rattled in their shells. Women harvested their fields and gathered crab apples, along with the last of the blackberries, before the first chill winds from the west swept over them. In winter, the jagged pines were silhouetted against the purple sky, and the snows fell steadily, filling the valleys and spreading a soft white blanket over the land. Frozen rivers and lakes disappeared under the drifts, and people settled around their longhouse fires, trudging only short distances in their snowshoes.

Whatever the time of year, the Iroquois imbued their world with spiritual meaning. Above in the **Sky World** lived the right-handed twin, who was the Master of Life (also known as He Who Holds Up the Sky and Great Creator). In the Sky World, too, were Our Grandmother the Moon and Our Elder Brother the Sun. The land itself rested on the back of the turtle. The corn spirits watched over the villages and fields, and the little people and masked spirits dwelled in the forest. Below the land lived Flint, the evil, left-handed twin of the Master of Life—devious and stubborn, his body covered with sores.

The forest was the domain of men—hunters and warriors—who trotted along paths beneath the canopy of branches. Only faint shafts of light filtered through the leaves of the towering trees, whose trunks stood like columns holding up a high green ceiling. There was little brush on the forest floor, just a cushion of leaves or pine needles underfoot. It was a dim world, cool and nearly silent.

The **clan mothers** ruled the clearings where the villages and fields were found. Here, the earth absorbed the heat of the sun glinting brightly in the clear blue sky. The open places rang with the laughter of children and the talk of women working around the longhouses. The forest reached into the unknown, while the clearing was familiar and secure—it was home.

Whether forest or clearing, all the earth was like the air, necessary for survival but belonging to no one. The Iroquois never imagined that land could be bought and sold. As they encountered more and more settlers later in their existence, many Iroquois discovered that very different views on the land could be taken and enacted.

Samuel de Champlain drew this image of his encounter with the Iroquois tribes in 1609.

The Iroquois and Their Rivals

The Iroquois vigorously defended their lands from surrounding tribes. To the north in Canada lived the

Huron, who became rival traders and enemies of the Iroquois, as well as allies of the French. West of the Iroquois were the Tobacco tribe and the Neutrals, so called because they tried to stay out of the wars between the Iroquois and the Huron. The Susquehanna, or Conestoga, lived in what is now central Pennsylvania, along with the Erie tribe. As the Iroquois established themselves, they eventually drove out these Native American groups and others. Many Iroquois enemies were moved from their territories between the Adirondack Mountains and Niagara Falls farther west, to the Midwestern and Southern United States.

The Iroquois Confederacy

The Iroquois had their own language, and many Native American tribes spoke it. However, only five northeastern tribes became part of a powerful group of Iroquois, referred to as the Iroquois Confederacy. The Iroquois Confederacy began between 1570 and 1600. The five original tribes, or nations, and their location, east to west, were the Mohawk, Oneida, Onondaga, Cayuga (pronounced kigh-YOU-gah), and Seneca. The center of the Confederacy was in Onondaga country near present-day Syracuse, New York. Around 1722, the Tuscarora became the sixth member of the Confederacy after white settlers drove them from present-day Virginia and North Carolina. Together, the groups made up the Six Nations of the Iroquois. As years passed and the Six Nations grew in numbers, these tribes expanded their territory around the lower Great Lakes of Huron, Ontario, and Erie, as well as Lake Champlain and Lake George. They also settled along

The Iroquois Confederacy endured fighting with the French from the late 1600s to the mid 1700s.

the St. Lawrence River, primarily in what are now the provinces of Ontario and Quebec in Canada. Some branches of the League eventually extended as far west as Wisconsin and as far south as the Allegheny Mountains in Pennsylvania. At the height of its population in 1680, there were between ten thousand and seventeen thousand individual members in the Iroquois Confederacy.

Characteristics

Although there were many differences among the tribes of the League, the Iroquois spoke basically the same language and shared a similar way of hunting, gathering, farming, and waging war. Strong and agile, the Iroquois were somewhat taller than other North Americans as well as Europeans at the time of their first encounter. They had no written language, other than the **wampum** belts on which they recorded their history, so they relied on their excellent memories. They were able to vividly recall stories and long speeches, word for word, many years after hearing them.

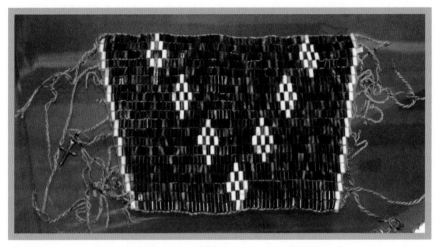

This wampum wrist ornament, circa 1700s, was most likely made and worn by the Iroquois.

The Iroquois valued courage, strength, endurance, and independence. They could be very cruel to their enemies, yet gentle, considerate, and highly cooperative among their own people. In large villages of a thousand or more people, they worked together constructing longhouses and providing for each other. Like other Native peoples of North America, they felt a spiritual kinship with the natural world. Although they hunted animals and gathered plants, they did not try to dominate their environment but found a place for themselves among all living things.

Storytelling

Part of the Iroquois' rich culture offered them the opportunity to memorize stories and tell them in great detail. Here is one story about the formation of the Iroquois:

Long ago, before the earth came to be, a husband and wife, who were expecting a child, lived in the Sky World. In the center of the Sky World stood a great tree with four white roots stretching north, south, east, and west, in the directions of the wind. It was a sacred tree, not to be touched by anyone, from which grew many kinds of leaves, fruits, and flowers. One day, the woman was gathering seeds and berries but also desired some bark from the root of the tree. She persuaded her husband to scrape the bark for her, but as he dug at the root, the floor of the Sky World collapsed. Gazing into the opening, the husband and wife were astonished that, far below, there was only water and the creatures who could live in or on it. Bending down for a closer look, the woman lost her balance and fell through the hole in the sky. She was caught by a flock of swans, which, flying wing tip to wing tip, made a feathery raft and carried her aloft.

But there was no land, only water below in which swam the fish and animals. The woman could neither fly nor swim, and the birds didn't know what to do with her. Finally, a turtle swam up and said, "There is room on my back." So the swans gently placed her on its shell. Realizing that there must be earth on which the woman could live, the creatures of the world below plunged deep into the water searching for soil. Again and again they dove, but only the muskrat, its lungs nearly bursting, was able to reach the bottom and bring up a little mud in its paws.

"Place the earth on my back," the turtle said. The muskrat did so, and the woman began to walk in a circle, in the same direction as the sun. The mud grew and grew until it became **Turtle Island**, which is the Iroquois name for their home in North America. The woman dropped the seeds and berries she had carried from the Sky World, and they sprouted into the plants and trees that now cover the earth. The children of the woman later became the Hodenosaunee, which means "people of the longhouse." This is what the Iroquois call themselves, and how the land and people came to be.

The history of the Iroquois is riddled with war, intrigue, and triumph. It is a story that persists in the modern day. The name Iroquois is remembered by many, Native and non-Native alike. Fiercely determined to keep their territory, the Iroquois did what they had to in order to protect it.

Hiawatha (*right*) helped form the Iroquois Confederacy with Deganawida.

We need to all work together as ... the tribe of Human Kind ... to make this world a good place for all.

—Howard Lyons, Mohawk Wolf Clan member

BUILDING A CIVILIZATION

No more than fifty or so people lived in the first Iroquois villages. The first villagers farmed crops and lived off the land around them. Sometimes, however, some tribes, such as the Mohawk, resorted to eating their own people. They often attacked neighboring tribes. This situation changed, though, with the arrival of Deganawida, said to be a member of the Huron tribe. Known as the Great Peacemaker, he is attributed with advising Hiawatha, an Onondaga member living with the Mohawk who became a great Iroquois leader, to cease his ways of living and instead adopt a different form of government. Deganawida had gone to many other Iroquois tribes, proclaiming peace. Eventually, he and Hiawatha started the Iroquois Confederacy. Between 1570 and 1675, the prime recruitment years of the Iroquois Confederacy, village populations grew to several hundred people, and in some cases, as many as three thousand lived in one village.

The Iroquois Confederacy formed as a means to keep peace between previously warring nations. The Five Nations forming the confederacy—Onondaga, Oneida, Mohawk, Cayuga, and Seneca tribes—kept peace for some three hundred years.

Life in an Iroquois Tribe

Larger Iroquois villages often lay on high ground for protection from attack, near streams where fresh drinking water could be found. As farmers, the Iroquois did not have to move continually like the hunting people of the plains. However, the village had to be moved every ten to fifteen years, when the soil of the fields became exhausted and game was scarce.

High log fences called palisades surrounded each village. With sharp points extending skyward, the logs were set into the ground and lashed together to create a fortress. Along the inside of the walls were high platforms where lookouts could warn villagers of enemy attack. Sometimes, the Iroquois designed entrances as a maze to confuse enemies and slow their progress into the village. Within the palisades, they constructed a number of large

Corn, a valuable crop, was kept in barrels made from trees to keep dry and to keep out animals, such as rodents.

dwellings called longhouses, as well as storage buildings and sweat lodges. They set up racks for drying and stretching animal hides and dug pits for burying garbage.

Villages were often quite large; many had 30 to 150 longhouses. They were lively places, filled with the bustling sounds of work—the thud of mortar and pestle as women ground corn, the scrape of flint blades on deer hides, and the chop of a stone ax. There was the crackle of the fires, and the air was tinged with the smell of wood smoke. Clanspeople enjoyed living and working together. Within the longhouses, they gladly shared food and fire.

Clans

There were ten **clans** among the people of the longhouse: Turtle, Bear, Wolf, Beaver, Deer, Hawk, Ball, Heron, Snipe, and Eel. Not all clans were represented in every nation—only the Turtle, Bear, and Wolf were found in all five nations of the original Iroquois Confederacy. All the people in a clan considered themselves related, even if they were originally from a different nation, and they remained members of their clan, or "longhouse family," for life. Children of all families in the clan grew up as brothers and sisters, and a large clan might occupy several longhouses in the village. The men in the clan hunted together in the forest while the women and children worked as a group in the garden.

The Longhouse

About 80 to 150 feet (24.2 to 45.7 meters) long and 20 to 30 feet (6.1 to 0.9 m) wide, a longhouse had a curved roof and a low entrance at each end either fitted with a bark door and wooden hinges or hung with the skins of deer or bear. A carving of the animal

The tribes of the Iroquois built longhouses in which they lived with their clans.

representing the clan living in the longhouse was mounted above the doorway so that visitors from other villages could find shelter among their own people. Usually built in late spring or early summer, longhouses were made of wooden poles covered with shingles of elm bark. Saplings lashed to the frame held down the bark. To waterproof the longhouse, cracks in the bark were sealed with sticky sap from spruce trees. There was a row of smoke holes in the curved roof, each of which was covered with a piece of bark that could be nudged aside with a pole from inside the longhouse.

Fifteen to twenty families lived in each longhouse. A center aisle ran the length of the impressive building, separating the families on either side and providing a place for eight to ten fire pits used for cooking and heat. After 1700, the Iroquois built smaller longhouses with three to four fire pits, housing fewer families because of population loss from disease and war. Council meetings were also held in these central spaces, or in special longhouses reserved for ceremonies.

Set about 4 feet (1.2 m) off the ground, platforms for sleeping and storing personal belongings were built along the inside walls of the longhouse. Sheets of elm bark were used to divide the space into compartments. Overhead, a bright tapestry of red, yellow, and purple braided corn, dried squash, and smoked meat hung from the rafters and crossbeams, along with items such as snowshoes and **cradleboards**. The typical Iroquois longhouse also held clay pots for cooking and carrying water, wooden bowls for serving food, burden straps for cradleboards, sharpened bone tools, and perhaps a deer jaw used to scrape dried corn kernels from cobs or a birch-bark storage chest acquired by trade with the Algonquin. Pots, kettles, baskets, clothes, weapons, and other possessions were kept on the platform. Squash and other foods might also be stored on the ground under the platform or in bins made of hollow logs.

People slept on cornhusk mats, covering themselves in the winter with bearskins to keep themselves warm against the wind blowing through the cracks between the elm bark shingles.

Government

Iroquois government was based on the clans. Within each longhouse lived an extended family, called the **ohwachira**, whose members were related through the female line. The oldest woman in the ohwachira, known as the clan mother, served as the leader. She supervised farming and the other group work of the women.

Iroquois religious ceremonies followed the seasons and the cycles of the moon, and the clan mother was responsible for bringing people together at the appropriate time. It was she who settled disputes within the longhouse, and in consultation with other women, selected the **sachem**, or leader, who represented the clan in the village council. She also advised the sachem and made sure he followed the Great Law that bound the nations together in the League.

A sachem generally served for life, unless he displeased his clan mother or was impeached. He was then removed or symbolically "dehorned." This meant that his traditional antler headdress, awarded to each sachem upon being installed, was taken away from him. When a sachem died, it was the clan mother along with the other women who named a successor. All adult members of the clan voted on her choice. If approved, the new sachem assumed the name and position of his predecessor.

An Iroquois girl named Pretty Face is dressed in traditional Iroquois costume, circa 1927.

The People and Culture of the Iroquois

The village council discussed practical matters of hunting, fishing, farming, defense, religion, and ceremonies. Women did not participate directly in this council but headed households and exercised great influence over the men. The tribe, or nation, was made up of all the villages within the territory and was represented by a council of the sachems from each of the clans. The tribal council discussed policy but lacked the authority to carry out decisions unless a consensus, or unanimous agreement, had been reached. Individual families, clans, and villages could refuse to take part in an attack on an enemy or any other action with which they disagreed.

Wartime Practices

During the years before the formation of the League, there was constant, bloody warfare among the five tribes—the Iroquois, or Haudenosaunee, were formidable warriors. French explorers had a saying: "They approach like foxes, fight like lions, and disappear like birds."

The Iroquois were notorious for their treatment of captives. Often, the Iroquois tortured them, and occasionally they practiced cannibalism, eating a particularly resilient captive's heart to acquire some of his courage. Some captives—mostly women and children—were adopted into the tribe, usually to replace family members who had been killed. The others were forced to run a **gauntlet** in which they were beaten and jabbed by every man, woman, and child in the village, then tortured—often for days. Torture was undertaken partly to prove the mettle of the captive. He was seen as courageous if he chanted his **death song**, without crying out, even as his fingers were chopped off and his flesh burned.

The Great Peacemaker

Eventually, the five warring tribes declared a truce among themselves and became among the best organized of Native American nations. Their political life was centered around the League, which was established about 1570 by Deganawida, who visited each of the tribes and encouraged unity, and the Mohawk leader Hiawatha, or Hayenwatha, whose name means "he who seeks the wampum belt."

Henry Wadsworth Longfellow mistakenly used the name for the hero of his famous poem "The Song of Hiawatha." The Hiawatha in the poem is actually based on Manabozho, a mythical figure of the Ojibwa people. In the mid-1800s, Henry Rowe Schoolcraft, a government agent in the upper Great Lakes, began collecting Ojibwa folklore and legends, including tales about Manabozho. He also acquired stories of Hiawatha, from New York author J. V. H. Clark, for his book *Notes on the Iroquois*. However, in his book, Schoolcraft confused Hiawatha with Manabozho, and Longfellow thus ascribed many legends to Hiawatha instead of Manabozho. According to legend, Manabozho dwelled in the skies but came to live with the Onondaga, the most favored tribe of the Iroquois. The real Hiawatha was a great Iroquois statesman who taught his people the art of good living—friendship, farming, and good will—and joined with Deganawida in creating the League.

"ON HIS HEAD HIS EAGLE FEATHERS,
ROUND HIS WAIST HIS BELT OF
WAMPUM."
THE SONG OF HIAWATHA
LONGFELLOW.

This illustration features in Henry Longfellow's poem "The Song of Hiawatha," circa 1885. Myths of Hiawatha are often confused with those of an Ojibwa chief named Manabozho.

Building a Civilization

According to legend, Deganawida, who is reverently referred to only as the Great Peacemaker by the Iroquois, traveled in a canoe of glistening white stone from his birthplace in Ontario, Canada, to the warring tribes of New York. He showed how one arrow could easily be broken. He then bound five arrows together and said, "If the five nations can come together and live in peace, like this bundle of arrows, then you will be very strong—so strong that this union will last forever." In the story, he also uprooted a towering white pine tree, called the Tree of Peace, and told the men to throw their weapons into the hole. Then he replanted the Tree of Peace, with the weapons forever buried underneath it. At the top of the tree he placed an eagle to screech a warning if danger ever threatened the tree, and at its foot he extended four White Roots of Peace. "If any person or nation of people desires to live in peace," he explained, "they may find one of the Roots and follow it back to the Tree of Peace."

Although much of Hiawatha's life is now obscured by legend, around 1570 he and Deganawida established the Iroquois Confederacy. Since Deganawida had a speech impediment, Hiawatha preached the message of unity as he traveled among the tribes. Initially, he was strongly opposed, especially by Atotarho, a powerful Onondaga sachem.

According to legend, Atotarho had snakes growing out of his head and turtle claws for hands and feet. Despite a crippled body, he had supernatural powers—and he bitterly opposed the alliance of Iroquois nations. To gain Atotarho's support, Hiawatha had to comb the snakes out of his hair and straighten his body and spirit. Atotarho also insisted on several conditions, including that the Onondaga serve as hosts at the annual meeting of the Great Council and that they be allowed more representatives at council than any other tribe. The Onondaga were also to keep the wampum belt that was the record of the meeting and maintain the council fire that burned continually in their village. Atotarho's name became the official title of the hereditary chief.

This confederacy ended generations of warfare and became a model for the United States government. No one knows what happened to Hiawatha after the League of the Iroquois was established.

Maintaining Peace

The Mohawk, who were the first to accept the Great Peace and join the League, became known as the Elder Brothers. Vowing to keep peace among themselves, the five tribes founded a council of fifty sachems whose names, including Deganawida, Hiawatha, and Atotarho, have been passed down through the ages. There were nine each from the Mohawk and Oneida, fourteen from the Onondaga, ten from the Cayuga, and eight from the Seneca. The seat of Deganawida was always left vacant, making the number of sachems forty-nine in practice. Gifted men and women who had distinguished themselves also participated as a group of advisors called the Pine Tree Sachems. Although they weren't allowed to vote at council, these sachems did have the right to speak in meetings. Even if they acted contrary to the laws of the Great Peace, they could not be removed from the council, but no one would listen to their words.

These leaders met every summer in the land of the Onondaga, who came to be known as the Keepers of the Council Fire. The meeting opened with a prayer offered by the Onondaga and a thanksgiving address. These meetings lasted for several days, as sachems debated "across the fire." Because the sachems all had to agree to "speak with one voice," they often made long and eloquent speeches to persuade others in the council. As each sachem spoke, he held the strings of wampum to show that he was speaking truthfully from the heart. When the wampum was passed to another, it indicated that the truth of his words had been accepted.

The League was represented by a sacred circle and strings of wampum on the belt made with 1,800 beads or shells. The fifty strings on the wampum stood for each of the sachems. One string was slightly longer to show that the Onondaga were the Keepers of the Wampum. Wampum, which comes from the Algonquin word for "white bead," was often traded or received as a gift. The beads that glowed white indicated the harmony of being right and positive, while black or purple represented the opposite: destruction and even death. Europeans sometimes used strings or belts of wampum instead of coins, but the Iroquois never used wampum as money. Wampum belts were used to call sachems to council, and they were sent to other tribes as an invitation to join a war. Treaties between tribes and with Europeans were recorded on wampum belts. They also became a kind of writing on which Iroquois history and the meetings of the League were recorded.

Each member of the council was equal, but one chief had the authority to light the Great Council fire, or call them together. The individual members kept their power through votes and vetoes, since all leaders had to agree to a decision. The nations in the League didn't actually unite in battle against their enemies, such as the Huron, but they kept the Great Peace with each other for over three hundred years. If blood was shed within the League, instead of revenge, the victim's family was compensated with wampum or other payment of goods set by the League or tribal council. Anyone who repeatedly committed crimes, such as treason or theft, was banished from the tribe. He or she no longer had a home or family for protection.

The Great Longhouse

The Iroquois viewed the League as a great longhouse, extending east to west over their land. Like a longhouse, the League contained many fires, one for each tribal family, but, like the members of a clan, they were to live together in peace. The beams of the longhouse represented each of the tribes and the rafters symbolized the laws that sheltered them. The entrances at each end were guarded; the Mohawks were known as the Keepers of the Eastern Door, and the Seneca as the Keepers of the Western Door.

At one time, the Iroquois thought they could bring the Great Peace to all nations of the world, including the European settlers. The Iroquois Confederacy was a remarkable form of democratic government with a system of laws "to strengthen the house" by assuring order and prosperity among its members. Benjamin Franklin, one of the architects of the American republic, praised the league. He used it as an example of

The Council House was an important building in which members of the Iroquois Confederacy gathered to discuss actions and make decisions.

cooperation when he argued in favor of a strong union of states.

In the end, the Iroquois idea of peace did not exvtend to other Native groups outside the Confederacy. As the Iroquois grew to be more capable, exacting

The People and Culture of the Iroquois

warriors, they fought fiercely with other tribes and eventually with European settlers to protect their land and resist change to their communities. As a result, their dominance drove many Native groups out of the area and onto other, distant lands.

Iroquois villages were made up mostly of longhouses, such as these.

CHAPTER THREE

There are no secrets. There is no mystery. There is only common sense.

—Onondaga Tribe saying

LIFE IN THE IROQUOIS NATION

The Iroquois had many rituals accompanying different stages in their lives. From birth to death, special rituals and practices were performed. These are some of the traditions celebrated by the Iroquois.

The Life Cycle

Men, women, and children had different tasks to perform during the different stages of life. A man proved himself in battle, while a woman demonstrated courage and strength during childbirth. Midwives assisted mothers so that their babies came safely into the world. Children grew up within the warm glow of their families, knowing they had a place within the clan. Adults learned to provide food, clothing, and shelter for themselves and to share with others in the village. The dead, whether young or old, were honored in ceremonies that helped them make their way into the afterlife.

Being Born

When a woman was about to have a baby, she moved to a special hut, along with an experienced older woman from her longhouse. The woman knelt on a deerskin and held onto a pole as the baby was born. If she cried or made any kind of noise during labor, she was scolded for not being brave.

The birth of a girl was considered a great blessing, because she could eventually bear more clan members and continue the cycle of generations. When a boy was born, he was washed in a nearby stream or in the snow to make him strong and courageous. Babies were given a taste of animal oil to cleanse their bodies and to feed the guardian spirit that the Iroquois believed came to live in the soul from the moment of birth.

Babies received a name from the clan mother, which was confirmed at the next village festival. Over the years, the child would receive a succession of names. All the names belonged to the clan, and none were held by two living people at the same time.

The newborn was wrapped in animal skins and strapped to a cradleboard, with sphagnum moss or

An illustration of an Iroquois man and woman.

cattail fluff used for a diaper. Highly decorated with clan symbols and other designs, cradleboards were about 2 feet (0.6 m) long with a hood on top to shield the baby's face from sun and rain. At night, babies slept with their parents or in a nearby hammock made of animal skins.

When the baby was a few days old, the mother and child returned to the shelter of the longhouse. Mothers took up their work as soon as possible, carrying their babies along with them. A piece of leather, called a burden strap, was attached to the cradleboard and wrapped around the mother's forehead, holding the baby firmly in place. Mothers often hung the cradleboards from a tree or stood them up in a corner of the longhouse. Babies could then watch their mothers work in the cornfields or at the cooking fire.

Mothers nursed their babies for two or three years, gradually introducing a little corn soup and gruel into their diet. Living together in the longhouse family, the mother's sisters also helped in parenting, so each child had several mothers. As soon as they were strong enough, young children helped to fetch wood and water for their mothers. They carried the water in small jars. Boys stayed close to their mothers until age eight or nine, when they began to spend time with their own group of friends. They often formed close friendships that lasted a lifetime. Girls continued to work with their mothers and the other women of the village.

Growing Up

Parents were very fond of their children and rarely punished them. Typically, they threw water on a misbehaving child. In serious cases, they asked a person wearing a mask of Longnose, the cannibal clown, to jump out to scare the youngster. Children were not formally educated; however, storytelling was a means of both entertainment and instruction in the beliefs and ways of their people. During the winter months, the elders of the village told stories that included lessons about the history of their people and proper behavior.

Boys learned to hunt and fight from their fathers and uncles (their mother's brothers), as well as how to master various crafts essential to their survival. To develop their coordination, eyesight, and aim, boys practiced their skills with bow and arrow, blowgun, and tomahawk. They learned to catch fish in nearby streams and trap small animals in the forests. To prove his courage as a hunter and warrior, a boy was left alone in the forest to defend himself against wolves and bears. This usually happened during puberty. Over the course of his studying, a boy learned to "read" the land by recognizing an animal's track in the light snow.

The People and Culture of the Iroquois

Another ritual involving the forest was a vision quest. Around the same age, alone, without food, boys fasted for about two weeks to induce dreams to help them discover what they would become later in life. At some point, their guardian spirit revealed itself. The guardian spirit foretold the boys' future and left them with a special song. During times of danger, boys sang this song for courage and protection.

As girls came of age, the older women of the longhouse supervised them closely. When a girl had her first menstrual period, she was considered a danger to the welfare of the village and was isolated from others. Using special pots, the girl cooked and ate her food alone during this time of the month. She would do this every month until she married a young man from another clan. During each menstrual period, throughout their childbearing years, women followed these same practices.

Marrying

In some Iroquois tribes, a mother suggested a possible wife for her son. If the young man liked her choice, his mother spoke to the young woman's mother, who decided if he was a skilled enough hunter and warrior to marry her daughter. The clan mother made the final decision regarding the proposed union. She reviewed the couple's age, suitability, and clan relations. If she said no, the marriage could not take place; if the marriage was approved, the young man and woman marked their courtship by an exchange of gifts, but there was no dowry. For the marriage feast, the bride made corn bread, and the groom brought meat.

Families were very important to the Iroquois tribes. Lineage was traced through the mother's side of the family.

The Iroquois were different from Europeans in that the bride brought her husband home with her. Even after the marriage, the woman's bonds to her clan were stronger than those to her husband. He always remained a member of his own clan and a guest in her longhouse, whereas she spent her entire life among her own clan.

Couples ideally became joined for life, and divorce was viewed unfavorably. However, if a husband proved

The People and Culture of the Iroquois

lazy or unable to provide for his wife, she would order him to pick up his clothes, weapons, and blanket and leave the longhouse—or she simply placed his belongings outside the doorway. Each was then free to remarry.

Changing Death Rituals

Because of disease and war, the Iroquois did not enjoy long lives. As many as half the children died before they reached the age of twelve, and the average life-span for adults was just thirty-one years.

Burial practices varied by tribe and changed over time. Early on, the Iroquois honored their dead in elaborate funerals. They placed the bodies on wooden scaffolds high above the ground so they would be closer to the divine forces in the sky. The deceased remained on the scaffold until the body decomposed. Then the bones were bundled and buried in a kind of mass grave called an **ossuary**. There was usually one burial place for each village. In later times, the deceased was dressed in "dead clothes" and buried in a curled-up position in a bark-lined grave about 3 feet (1 m) deep with items such as food, clothes, and weapons needed for survival in the afterlife. After contact with Europeans, the Iroquois began to bury their dead in wooden coffins.

Shortly after death, the home of the deceased was cleaned. Reflective objects were turned around so that no one, especially children, would be frightened by seeing an image of the ghost. Food was set out for the spirit of the dead person, and at least two people kept a vigil over the body.

The Iroquois would leave their dead on platforms until all that was left were their bones.

The Iroquois believed that the spirit of the departed lingered in the village for ten days. They held the Tenth Day Feast with offerings of food, tobacco, and song to protect the living and to sustain the deceased until its spirit reached the Land of the Dead beyond the setting sun. Twice a year, they held the Feast of the Dead to help any spirits still hovering about the village on their journey along the Milky Way, the Path of the Dead. Expressing the wishes of all the mourners, a speaker chanted, "I will make the sky clear for you."

Family Life

Iroquois society was matrilineal, meaning people traced their family tree through their mother's side of the family. Children were always considered part of their mother's clan. Should a man's wife die, he would be encouraged to marry one of her sisters so that remarriage would not disrupt the lineage of the family. Men had little role in managing the household, which was the exclusive responsibility of the women. In fact, everything inside the longhouse belonged to the women—even the longhouse itself. Men owned only their clothes, tools, and weapons.

Women were primarily responsible for rearing the children, often putting the girls and younger boys to work in the garden. When the boys turned eight or nine, they began to spend time with other boys and with male relatives—often their uncles—to learn the roles of men among the Iroquois. Expected to be physically strong, girls helped their mothers and aunts, learning by example how to take care of the home and fields.

Girls watched their mothers make pots by rolling wet clay into a ball and then making a dent with their fists. To shape the pot, they slapped the clay with a wooden paddle as they turned the pot on their fist. Women dried the pots in the sun, then baked them in a hot fire. They didn't glaze their pots, but made patterns with fingernails, corncobs, and sticks. Girls also learned to make cornmeal by placing yellow kernels in a hollowed-out log called a mortar and pounding it with a wooden mallet called a pestle. As the givers of life, women were responsible for feeding the people of the longhouse. Since women headed households, girls were encouraged to take a leading role in their families.

Crops

In early spring, girls helped their mothers collect milkweed, leeks, skunk cabbage, and other tender greens to supplement their diet after the long winter. During the Berry Moon of June, at the beginning of summer, they gathered wild strawberries and celebrated the arrival of the first fruit of the year. They also picked wild plums, grapes, cherries, and crab apples along with chestnuts, black walnuts, and hickory nuts.

When the oak leaves grew to the size of a red squirrel's paw, the girls and women piled the earth into hills in communal fields. They planted seeds that had been soaked in water to make them sprout more readily. As a group, the women planted corn, beans, and squash—crops so interrelated and essential to Iroquois survival that they were called "the **three sisters**." When grown together, corn, beans, and squash kept the garden plot in balance, which was very important to all aspects of Iroquois life. Beans returned nitrogen to the soil, corn provided stalks on which the bean vines climbed, and the broad squash leaves—whether Hubbard, crookneck, or winter squash—spread over the ground to shade out weeds. Women also planted sunflowers, whose seeds could be easily stored.

Much of the autumn harvest was saved to provide food through the long winter. Women smoked or dried meat, which was stored high up in the longhouse. Corn was either hung in the longhouse or kept in a crib, a small building with open slats, which allowed air to flow around the brightly colored ears of corn. Settlers later adapted similar designs for corncribs on their farms.

RECIPE

CORN SOUP

Here is a recipe for corn soup, which was often part of the daily meal in Iroquois longhouses. Traditionally, this recipe was made with dried white corn (large, flat kernels) that was boiled in ashes to make **hominy**. The hominy was then rinsed and cooked with deer meat and beans.

In this modern version, you can substitute canned hominy corn and salt pork, cooked ham, or another meat of your choice.

INGREDIENTS

2 19-ounce (540-milliliter) cans of hominy corn
1 pound (453 grams) of diced salt pork or cooked ham
1 pound (450 mL) of dried kidney beans

Place the hominy corn, salt pork, and kidney beans in a large pot. Add enough water to cover the ingredients and simmer for 1.5 to 2 hours until the beans are tender. Add salt and pepper to taste.

Dried corn was also roasted to make parched corn, which stored well and provided excellent nutrition. Parched corn was placed in bark barrels and stored in pits in the ground, along with pumpkins and other kinds of squash.

Cooking and Making Crafts

Girls helped their mothers prepare meals over fires in the center aisle of the longhouse, roasting or boiling fish and wild game. They boiled water by dropping hot stones from the fire directly into clay pots. Corn was their most important source of food, and they grew several kinds, including white flint, or squaw corn, and dent corn. Green ears of corn were boiled or roasted; sometimes kernels were scraped from the cob and fried in bread or used in soups. Corn soup was a favorite dish, as was **succotash**, a mixture of beans, corn, and hominy. To make hominy, the Iroquois boiled corn with wood ashes to loosen the hulls. Sometimes they ground the kernels of corn with a mortar and pestle and then mixed the cornmeal with maple sugar, dried berries, or chopped dried meat. People also ate corn in puddings and bread, which was often flavored with dried nuts or berries, and in soup made from strawberries and green corn. Women used gourd ladles to scoop food out of the cooking pots. People ate with wooden spoons and bowls and drank from cups made from turtle shells or carved from wood. They usually had only one meal a day, but a clay pot was always on the fire, and they could eat whenever they got hungry.

Women also grew corn to provide many kinds of useful materials. Corn cakes were wrapped in corn leaves, then cooked. The juice from green stalks was applied to cuts and bruises. Dry stalks were hollowed out and plugged, then used to store medicines. Stalks were also used as toy spears and clubs. Rough cobs made good scrub brushes and stoppers for jugs, and dried yellow kernels were used as beads in rattles. Women shredded cornhusks to make filling for pillows and mattresses or wove husks into trays, baskets, mats, and slippers. Mothers made cornhusk dolls with corn silk hair for their daughters, and men fashioned ceremonial masks from the dried leaves.

The Iroquois crafted elaborate jewelry and boxes, such as this one, made of wood and porcupine quills.

In addition to farming and cooking, women crafted fine pottery and splint baskets to furnish their longhouses. They also made a versatile twine from the inner bark of elm trees. They cut the bark into narrow

Iroquois women made clothing from animal furs, hides, and deerskin.

strips, which they boiled in ashes and water to separate into threads. Men wove the threads into fishnets, and with bone needles, women knitted the threads into lovely and useful burden straps. Women wore these straps around their heads to support cradleboards, food baskets, and wooden frames called **burden carriers** on their backs.

Women also made the buckskin clothing for the clan. First they tanned the deerskin—a long and difficult task that took ten to twelve days. After the deer was skinned, all the hair had to be scraped from the hide. The hide was then cleaned with a solution of hardwood ashes—which contain lye—and boiling water. The deer's brain, liver, and fat were boiled to release an oil, and the mixture was rubbed into the skin to soften it. The hide was then stretched on a rack and dried, after which it was smoked. Smoking toughened the buckskin and gave it a pleasing tan color.

Women gathered pieces of buckskin and sewed them together to make moccasins, **breechcloths**, and skirts. In warm weather, boys and men wore only a breechcloth, a piece of buckskin run between their legs and tied around their waists. Girls and women wore a knee-length skirt. During the winter, males added a jerkin, or buckskin shirt, leggings, and sometimes a kilt-like skirt. Girls and women also wore shirts and leggings as well as a longer skirt. During the winter, men and women wrapped themselves in robes of moose, bison, and bearskins with the fur turned inward for greater warmth.

Clothing not only offered protection but served as a form of decoration. Women often adorned finished clothing with porcupine quills and dyed moose hair. Feathers, fur, shells, bones, claws, wood, and stones such as quartz were made into jewelry and hair ornaments, many of which had religious meaning. Both men and women wore necklaces, bracelets, and earrings. During the summer, they smeared their bodies with bear grease to protect themselves from mosquitoes and blackflies. Mixing red ochre, bloodroot, and charcoal with sunflower seed oil, they also painted themselves with geometrical designs or animal figures. Men painted their faces as well—blue for health, black for war or mourning, and red for either life or violent death—and they tattooed their bodies. Women and girls braided their hair, which was allowed to grow long. Men usually went bareheaded. Some shaved one side of their head and let a long lock hang down from the other. Others shaved both sides of their heads, leaving a ridge of hair—called a scalp lock or roach—on top, running from the hairline to the nape of their necks, which is popularly known today as a "Mohawk."

Once Europeans arrived and began to trade with the Iroquois, the Iroquois style of dress changed. Settlers brought new materials, such as wool and linen, and many Native people saw the benefit of making clothing out of these more durable, comfortable pieces that could be sewn more easily than buckskin. From this time onward, the Iroquois generally adopted the same fashions as the settlers. Brightly colored solids and later calicos and prints were especially popular among the women, who added ribbons and woven sashes with glass beads embroidered onto the cloth in lovely floral patterns. Glass beads became the most common material for jewelry.

Hunting

During early summer, when elm bark was most easily stripped from the tree, men built or repaired longhouses and made canoes. Many Native Americans of the Northeast used birch-bark canoes, but the Iroquois made their canoes of elm bark. They stripped large pieces of bark from the trees and removed the rough outer layer, then they joined the sheets over a frame of ash wood to form a pointed canoe. An ash wood rim was run around the edge of both sides and lashed together with bark twine. The canoes ranged in length from 12 to 40 feet (3.7 to 12.2 m). The biggest canoes carried up to twenty warriors and were mainly used on lakes and large rivers. Smaller canoes carried two or three people on journeys with frequent portages. Although sturdy and well made, Iroquois canoes were thick, heavy, and slow. Whenever possible, the Iroquois stole light, fast, birch-bark canoes from the Algonquin.

The men cleared fields for the women in preparation for planting. The only crop grown by men was tobacco, which they smoked with sumac leaves and red willow bark. This sacred plant was believed to be a means of speaking with the spirit world, and its smoke rose to the skies during most village ceremonies. Tobacco was sprinkled on rapids to quiet the spirits living in the rivers, and small bags were attached to masks to strengthen their magic.

Men made snowshoes and household utensils and collected bones, antlers, stone, and wood to make tools. Most tool blades were shaped from a type of flint called chert. A durable stone on which a very sharp edge could be chipped, or knapped, chert was used to make points for arrows and spears, as well as blades for axes, scrapers, knives, and other tools. With stone hammers, the men knocked off bits of flint to form the general shape of the point or blade. They then used deer antlers to chip sharp edges on the blade and notches for tying the tool to a handle or the point to the shaft. Men also made tomahawks and war clubs from pieces of flint or other stones strapped to wooden handles. Hardwoods, especially hickory, maple, and cherry, were often used for weapon shafts and tool handles. Chert was also used for such items as fishnet sinkers and small hammers.

Deer and moose antlers, as well as bones, were honed into the points of arrows or spears, hair combs, musical instruments, and farming tools; the shoulder blade of the deer or a tortoise shell attached to a stick made a good hoe. Fishhooks, needles, and many other objects were fashioned from small bones, and men used sinew—the tendons in animal muscles—as a very tough string to tie arrow points to the wooden shaft. Cord was also made from strips of bark and plant stems. Tools were held tightly together with glue made from boiled fish scales and other animal parts.

In addition to repairing longhouses and making tools, the men protected their villages during times of warfare, but they were often away from home for months attacking distant tribes. In fact, most of the important tasks of the men—hunting, fighting, and trading—were undertaken away from the longhouses. The Iroquois did not have horses. Men either paddled canoes down rivers or jogged along trails, making temporary camps in the forest. Trails connected one village clearing with another and were used continually for travel and communication. A major trail that ran east to west became the backbone of the trail network— the corridor in the great "longhouse" of the Iroquois Confederacy. Along this trail, the Iroquois went "from fire to fire" or "from smoke to smoke" visiting other tribes. The Iroquois also followed trails into the forest for purposes of hunting and warfare.

To provide venison and other meat for their village, men hunted in the forests with bows and arrows for large game—mainly deer, black bear, elk, moose, and beaver. Deer was the primary source of meat in their diet. Bear was also prized for its greasy meat, which was used as ceremonial food, and for its thick hide, which was turned into warm blankets. Cooked beaver tail was considered a special delicacy.

Men shaped bows of sturdy hickory and strung them with a length of twisted woodchuck hide. They made arrow shafts of maple tipped with flint or bone points and feathered at the notched ends. In later years, they used blowguns to shoot rabbits, squirrels, raccoons, porcupines, and other small animals. Men also trapped bears in deadfalls and rabbits in snares. The land abounded with game birds, including ducks, geese, wild turkeys, ruffed grouse, and passenger pigeons, and hunters were skilled at bringing down feathered quarry. Fishing with spears and basket traps, as well as hooks and lines, the men provided trout, salmon, bass, perch, whitefish, and eels for their clan.

Often, men hunted alone, staying out for days and living on parched corn mixed with sugar. This work required skill, patience, endurance, and a thorough knowledge of the habits of wild animals. Sometimes, a group of hunters built a V-shaped brush fence, 2 or 3 miles (3.2 to 4.8 kilometers) long on each side, and drove deer toward the narrow opening, where they were shot by hunters hidden in the bushes. As many as a hundred deer could be taken in this method.

In the autumn, men left their longhouses for several weeks to go hunting, taking shelter in temporary camps in the forest. When the constellation Pleiades reached its highest point at dusk, they knew it was the end of the season and time to return to the village.

The Iroquois were fierce fighters who built their own weapons, including tomahawks.

The People and Culture of the Iroquois

Weapons and War Parties

Iroquois warriors relied on three weapons: a bow, a tomahawk with a stone head, and a war club. One type of war club was made of ironwood with a thick knot on the end. Another had a deer's sharp horn attached to the end.

The raid was the most common type of combat. War parties of ten to a hundred men quietly crept up to an enemy village and ambushed people as they left for the day. The warriors killed the men, taking their scalps, captured the women, and then fled homeward. Sometimes, tribes engaged in pitched battles with up to two thousand warriors on each side. They went to war to avenge a murder or other crime, to further their own prestige and personal power, to defend their lands, and to acquire captives to replace lost relatives.

Trading

Iroquois men traded with other Native American tribes, although they never had as many established trade routes as other Native groups, such as the Huron. Traveling primarily on foot, they traded with the Susquehannock, Delaware, and other tribes along the Atlantic coast as far south as present-day Florida and as far west as the Mississippi River. They exchanged food, clothing, jewelry, tools, and musical instruments for shells and other items. They in turn swapped the shells for tobacco and other goods from the Neutral and Petun tribes.

When they encountered the French and Dutch in the early 1600s, the Iroquois began to trade animal skins—especially beaver pelts—for copper kettles, cloth, glass beads, and iron axes. They also traded for forged metal tools, which were highly prized because they were easier to work with and more durable than flint tools. Men also acquired firearms early on from the Swedes, the Dutch, and later the British. This enabled them to achieve great power during the colonial period of American history. Competition in the lucrative fur trade brought the Iroquois into greater conflict with other tribes in the so-called Beaver Wars. Men also had to travel greater distances from their longhouses and were not able to hunt or work as much around the village. Their long absences made it difficult for families to provide for themselves. Traders also introduced rum, which had a devastating effect on the Iroquois. Not only did the settlers bring goods previously unknown to the Iroquois, but French priests, such as the Jesuits, and other missionaries introduced new religions, in particular Christianity. This new faith would affect the Iroquois and many other Native tribes as the decades passed.

Games and Sports

In addition to trading, men loved to compete among themselves in contests and games, testing agility and endurance. Like other woodland dwellers, the Iroquois needed to be able to run fast, so boys often had races. They practiced with bows and arrows to develop their hunting skills, and they threw spears through a rolling hoop to improve their aim. Their favorite game was stickball, an early version of lacrosse. They played with a wooden stick that had a leather mitt at one end to catch and carry the ball, which was carved from wood or made of deerskin filled with hair. Games were hotly contested, even brutal, preparation for the rigors of battle, and many players were injured.

During the winter, the Iroquois played "snow snake," a game in which they skimmed a long, straight stick as far as possible over the snow. During the cold months, they also played games of chance and guessing games in the longhouse. One of the most popular was the Bowl Game (later called the Peach Stone Game after the introduction of the fruit). This game was played with a wooden bowl and six plum seeds, or stones, painted black on one side. Each player banged the bowl on the ground, making the stones jump and land with different sides facing up. The winner was the player who had the most plum stones with either the light or dark side turned up.

Girls and women, as well as boys and men, loved sports. A favorite game was shinny, which was played with a flattened buckskin ball. Any number of players divided into two teams. Each player had a stick that resembled a field hockey stick. Goalposts were set up at each end of a field, about 200 yards (183 m) long. The object of the game was to drive the ball between the other team's goalposts.

Over the centuries, the Iroquois developed a detailed, thriving civilization. With the help of traders in the 1600s, they quickly became expert marksmen. Their skills as warriors made them ferocious attackers against any Native tribe that tried to rival them.

The tribes of the Iroquois Confederacy held deeply rooted beliefs about nature and the wildlife that surrounded them.

CHAPTER FOUR

*They are not dead
who live in the hearts
they leave behind.*

—Tuscarora Tribe saying

BELIEFS OF THE IROQUOIS

The Iroquois had mixed beliefs. They were strongly connected to the land and respected what it had to offer, but they also believed in the power of dreams and the influence of the supernatural on everyday life. These beliefs continue today in the tradition of the Iroquois tribes.

The Iroquois believed in the power of dreams to tell the future and control events.

The Supernatural and Dreaming

The Iroquois believed that supernatural forces were present in all things in nature. These spirit forces were created by the supreme being. Sky spirits assumed the form of wind, thunder, sun, moon, and stars. Earth spirits were found in plants and animals. All these spirit forces flowed together in **orenda**, the force that controlled the weather and all living things. Flowing like a song through nature, orenda gave people spiritual power and the ability to undertake mighty deeds.

When men and women arose in the morning they thanked the Master of Life that they were alive for another day. According to tradition, the Master of Life was constantly engaged in a battle with his evil brother, Flint. The Iroquois believed that a balance between good and evil was necessary for harmony in the world. People were both good and bad, just as wolves were not completely wicked, and rabbits, which nibble young green shoots of corn, were not entirely good.

The Iroquois respected the power of dreams. They devoted a great deal of time to interpreting them and loved to play a game in which they guessed each other's dreams. The dreamer offered riddles as clues or hints. For example, that which "whistles in the wind" meant the corn spirit, and an object that "has holes, yet catches" was the net on a lacrosse stick. Dreams—the wishes of the soul—were meant to be fulfilled. People believed that anything they dreamed would actually happen to them, so if a warrior dreamed of being wounded, he would ask a friend to cut him slightly, making the dream come true in a harmless manner rather than as a serious injury in battle. Dreams and visions were also part of religious ceremonies. The shaman dreamed more than ordinary people and used the spirit forces that visited him in these dreams to cure illness.

The Iroquois respected the forests, the fields, and the rivers—their sources of food, clothing, and shelter. They held many rituals throughout the year before hunting and planting and said prayers of thanks that the earth had sustained them through another harvest. A hunter strove to think like the animal he stalked. By understanding the deer, he could more easily find it in the dense foliage and shadows of the woods. When he killed the animal, he knelt beside it and offered a prayer of thanks for its providing food and clothing for his family. Before he skinned the deer, he prayed that its spirit would be reborn and have a better life.

Medicine Societies

The people of the longhouse believed that illness had both a physical and spiritual cause, and they formed groups called medicine societies to protect themselves. They had great faith in these societies in healing the sick and battling evil. The most famous was the **False Face Society**, whose members wore carved wooden masks, such as "Old Broken-Nose," to frighten the spirits of disease. Members of the False Face Society performed the Traveling Rite each spring and fall to cleanse their village or to cure a person who was sick. They carved their masks out of a living tree, making offerings of tobacco smoke as they worked. They believed that if the carving was begun in the morning, the mask should be painted red; if begun

The False Face Society had many masks that represented faces its members had seen in dreams. This mask was used to help cure diseases.

in the afternoon, it should be painted black. When the mask was completed, it was cut from the tree. The group of healers came to the patient's longhouse, scraped their rattles on the walls, and screamed to scare away the evil spirits. Sometimes they were helped by another medicine society whose members wore cornhusk masks (also called "bushy head" or "fuzzy hair" masks). They danced, made tobacco offerings, and shook their rattles over the sick person.

Iroquois beliefs in healing and the spirit world are reflected in many of their stories. Here is one of their legends that has been told over the generations:

Deep in the past, a hungry old man, covered with sores, came to a village. At the longhouse of the Turtle Clan, he asked for food and shelter, but the matriarch was disgusted by the sight of him and told him to go away. Next, he went to the longhouse of the Beaver Clan but was turned away again. The Wolf, Deer, Eel, Heron, and Hawk Clans also refused to help him.

Tired, the old man came to the last longhouse in the village, which belonged to the Bear Clan. Here, the clan mother welcomed him and offered him food and a bed. The next day the old man became ill, but he told the woman of a secret plant that, if prepared in a special way, would cure him.

He got better, but over the next several weeks he became sick again and again, each day with a different illness. The woman gathered herbs and prepared them as he instructed, and each time he got better. Then one day the old man changed into a handsome warrior. He told the woman that he was the Great Spirit, and because she had been kind to him he had taught her all the cures for sickness.

Since that day only the women and men who belong to the Bear Clan, which became the Keeper of the Medicine, have known the cures for many illnesses.

Rituals and Celebrations

The Iroquois held many ceremonies, which closely followed the cycle of seasons. Each moon had a name. These names described either the season or the farming, hunting, gathering, or fishing that took place under that moon: Midwinter (February), Sugar (March), Fishing (April), Planting (May), Strawberry (June), Blueberry (July), Green Corn (August), Freshness (September), Harvest (October), Hunting (November), Cold (December), Very Cold (January). During seasonal ceremonies—the Midwinter, the Planting, the Green Corn, and the Harvest—people offered thanks and danced to rekindle both old and new dreams.

Each village had a special longhouse where councils were held and ceremonial speeches, songs, and dances were offered. There was much feasting as people danced to the beat of water drums and rattles and raised their voices in song. Drums were covered with a groundhog skin and filled with water, which gave the instrument a high, clear note. Rattles were made

Today, ceremonies and rituals of the Iroquois tribes are still celebrated. Here, Mohawk tribe members celebrate at a festival in Fonda, New York.

by filling turtle shells, horns, and elm bark pouches with seeds or pebbles. The most important were the turtle rattles made with the shells of snapping, box, or mud turtles. Men also tied strings of deer hooves to leather thongs and wrapped them around their knees. Tobacco was thrown on hot coals or smoked in stone or clay pipes, its smoke rising to the heavens. Pipes were smoked to welcome an honored guest or end disputes, but they were not passed from one person to another, as among plains tribes.

In the Midwinter Ceremony, masked messengers went through the longhouses, stirring the ashes of fires gone cold, to announce the start of the ceremony. The most important festival, the Midwinter, included a renewal of dreams, playing of games, and dancing.

Gourd rattles called pumpkin shakes were used to keep rhythm in the dances. Dream-guessing was an important part of the celebration as well. As with all Iroquois ceremonies, the Midwinter began and ended with a prayer giving thanks. The Iroquois did not ask the supreme being for anything, but expressed gratitude for what they had already been given.

In the early spring, when they tapped maple trees for their sweet sap, people feasted, sang, and danced in the Maple Ceremony. This festival included the interpretation and acting out of dreams, the confession of sins, and the burning of tobacco. Masks and wampum were potent symbols of the spirit world. In the Thunder Ceremony, held when storms first swept across the land in the spring, the Iroquois gave thanks for the rains needed for a good crop. In gratitude for the distant thunder, they sprinkled tobacco on the fire and enjoyed a war dance and sometimes a game of lacrosse. During the Planting Ceremony, they were filled with both hope and worry. Although they did not ask for good weather for their crops, the Iroquois made offerings of shell beads and tobacco in the hope of bringing rain. If the rains did not come, they might hold another Thunder Ceremony.

In June, the people of the longhouse held the Strawberry Ceremony in an atmosphere of good feeling. Tobacco was not necessary at this festival because strawberries grew within reach, and there was no need for fragrant smoke to rise skyward to the Great Spirit. Gratitude was deeply felt because of the warm weather and summer abundance. A delicious strawberry drink was a special treat.

The Strawberry Ceremony was one of the most important celebrations for the Iroquois.

Other seasonal festivals were the Green Bean Ceremony, the Green Corn Ceremony, and the Harvest Ceremony. The Green Corn Ceremony marked the time when sweet corn had ripened and was eaten. People gave thanks that the crops had been successfully harvested. Women played a central role in this ceremony, which had to do with food for the body and the spirit.

Both the Sun and the Moon Ceremonies were usually held during a long period of clear weather. People gave thanks to these heavenly bodies. The ceremony included shooting arrows at the sun in the day and at the moon at night, and tobacco was burned so that its smoke would rise to the skies.

The most important festivals were held at the first green of early summer, the autumn harvest, and the winter solstice. The Iroquois did all they could to ensure a good harvest and enough food to last the winter.

Between these events, people entertained themselves with outdoor games during the warm months. Throughout the bitter winter, they remained in their longhouses, eating corn, nuts, and dried vegetables, along with smoked meat and fish, and listening to stories. They had great respect for anyone who could ask a clever riddle, invent a word game, or tell a good tale.

Rituals of the Dead

Along with ceremonies to celebrate seasons and weather, and to heal the sick, there were rituals held for the dead. As mentioned in Chapter 3, the Iroquois believed in an afterlife. Their ways of treating the dead evolved with the times. However, one ceremony that has persisted through the ages is the Iroquois condolence ceremony. This ceremony, usually held to welcome in a new chief following an existing chief's death or to grieve the loss of a loved one, is estimated to have taken place within Iroquois tribes as far back as the 1500s. Once a five-day affair, condolence ceremonies today are usually one-day events, lasting six to seven hours. The idea of the condolence ceremony is to refresh one's mind and dispel negative thoughts, seeing a beloved one off to the afterlife.

Eagle feathers

The condolence ceremony involves the whole tribal community. The clans are divided into two parts, or moieties.

The Iroquois continue to celebrate traditions of the past. Here, an Iroquois tribe participates in a condolence ceremony at the Arlington National Cemetery in 2003.

One moiety consists of the clans from which the deceased originated. This side will be in mourning. A complimentary moiety will be the condolers, helping the mourning side to overcome its grief. Traditionally, the mourning group or family would be rewarded with a wampum belt at the end of the ceremony; however, in more recent years, songs, prayers, and materials such as eagle feathers have taken on the role of traditional wampum. This ceremony is still practiced today, especially among the Mohawk tribe.

Overall, the Iroquois held deeply rooted beliefs that shaped the way they lived their day-to-day life. The arrival of the Europeans tested their beliefs in many ways, but ultimately, their traditions prevailed into the modern day.

The Iroquois way of life changed when Europeans arrived in the 1600s.

CHAPTER FIVE

He who would do great things should not attempt them all alone.

—Seneca saying

OVERCOMING HARDSHIPS

The world of the Iroquois changed after they encountered Europeans in the early 1600s. Over the decades, the Iroquois way of life shifted in many ways. For example, by the late 1700s, the majority of Iroquois families were living in log cabins rather than in the traditional longhouse. They had likewise started to adopt Western ways of dressing and used European-style tools and weapons, such as the rifle. Before long, the Iroquois way of life would completely shift, influenced by everyday settlers, missionaries, and disease.

With Triumph, Change

In the mid-1600s, the Confederacy became very powerful when the Iroquois crushed the Huron tribes and then defeated the other tribes around them. The French had been trying unsuccessfully to conquer the Iroquois since Samuel de Champlain, a French explorer, had routed a Mohawk war party in 1609. By the middle of the 1700s, however, the Iroquois dominated all of New York and lower Canada—from the St. Lawrence River to the shores of Lake Erie.

From the time Europeans first arrived in North America, the world of the Iroquois had begun to change. Originally, the Iroquois viewed these new people as trading partners. Because of their powerful, well-established confederacy, they did not feel threatened by the Europeans. However, the pressure of war between the foreign powers eventually caused the tribes of the Confederacy to break their neutrality and to play a powerful role as the French and the English struggled for control of North America, especially around the Canadian border. Except for the Mohawk and Cayuga, who fell under the influence of Jesuit missionaries seeking to convert them to Christianity, the Iroquois sided with the British and were largely responsible for protecting the western flank of the English colonies from the French. The Iroquois Confederacy played a pivotal role in the British victory over the French in the French and Indian War (1754–1763), and after defeating the Illinois, Ojibwa, and other Great Lakes tribes, their power extended all the way to the Mississippi River. Yet many warriors were killed in these fierce battles. Smallpox and other diseases also reduced the Iroquois population, and settlers took more and more Iroquois land.

During the American Revolution (1775–1783), the Confederacy decided to remain neutral, but eventually the Tuscarora and Oneida supported "the thirteen fires," as they called the colonies, while the other tribes maintained "the bright chain of friendship" with the British. Warriors raided the American frontier to induce settlers to abandon their farms so that the revolutionary army would be denied provisions. The Iroquois League was thus split by a war that did not directly involve the member tribes, yet which cost them many lives. An old warrior recalled, "If all the skulls of the Oneida Indians killed by British forces in fighting to help the colonials get their freedom were piled together, the pile would be larger than the state capital in Albany." Thayendanegea, a Mohawk warrior also known as Joseph Brant, became a colonel in the British army and led troops into battle in the Revolutionary War.

Chief Joseph Brant, along with other Iroquois tribes, sided with the British during the American Revolution.

After the British lost the war, Brant led his people to safety in southern Ontario. They settled at Grand River, near the town of Brantford, named after their leader. Some members of the Cayuga tribe also moved to Canada following attacks by American troops. Another group of Cayuga stayed in the United States. Today, many Cayuga and Mohawk descendants live on the Grand River **Reservation** in the Canadian province of Ontario.

Finding a Place in a New World

In 1794, the Six Nations of the Iroquois signed the Treaty of Canandaigua. This agreement settled tensions between the United States and the Iroquois tribes by establishing peace. The treaty granted the Six Nations **sovereignty** over their own lands. However, not all of the nations benefited from this agreement. Over time, other treaties reduced the land of some Iroquois tribes, effectively pushing them from their territory. By 1807, some of the Cayuga that remained in the United States were moved to Sandusky, Ohio; in 1831, their reservation land was sold, so many had to move to Indian Territory in Oklahoma. More hardship awaited them on the journey to Oklahoma. More than one-third of the relocating Cayuga died before they reached the South. By 1838, many of the Oneida had relocated to Wisconsin. The Tuscarora were scattered, although a few found a home among the Mohawk. Red Jacket, the great Seneca leader, stated, "Your forefathers crossed the great water and landed on this island. Their numbers were small. We took pity on them, and they sat down among us. We gave them corn and meat. They gave us poison in return." The only tribes to remain close to their ancestral lands, in western New York, were the Seneca and the Onondaga, although their lands were greatly diminished in size throughout the 1800s and 1900s.

Dispersed, the Iroquois Confederacy had been torn apart by war, differences, and treaties. However, the original agreement of peace established between the Native nations remained. The tribes of the Confederacy settled in new areas of the continent and, in some cases, struggled to adjust to the new surroundings far from their homeland.

One of the enduring hardships of the resettlement process was being forced from their homeland and reestablishing a community. Many of the tribes were moved to reservations. These plots of land were not always located on manageable terrain, and some people struggled to adjust to new ways of farming and hunting, and different weather patterns.

Indian Industrial Schools

For the tribes of the Iroquois and many other Native groups sent to reservations, other difficulties existed in terms of schooling. Reservations provided education for children; however, many of these schools taught only in English. Boarding schools called Indian industrial schools were set up to educate Native American children in American ways. One of the most notorious industrial schools was the Carlisle Indian Industrial School in Carlisle, Pennsylvania. It educated hundreds of Native children during its life-span, including Iroquois children. By establishing these schools, the hope was to eliminate any trace of "nativeness." Many settlers considered Native people dangerous if left to their indigenous lifestyles. If American teachers were educating the students in American ways, Native people could assimilate into American culture more easily.

Many teachers were missionaries, men and women who tried to convert people to Christianity. These

This photograph of students in a chemistry class was taken at the Carlisle Indian Industrial School, circa 1915.

preachers had been in the United States since pre-colonial times and had succeeded in converting many Native people prior to the American Revolution. However, in the 1800s, a new push to convert people living on reservations began. Some Iroquois, such as the Oneida, did listen to the Christian teachings and were converted, but many others were hesitant to leave their old beliefs behind. Because of these peoples' determination, and the Iroquois ability to remember stories in great detail, the legends and teachings of the Iroquois tribes persist and continue today.

Handsome Lake and the Good Message

There were other religions established on the reservations. One such religion grew from a religious leader named Handsome Lake.

The People and Culture of the Iroquois

Around 1800, Handsome Lake, a member of the Seneca tribe, saw his people lose most of their land and his people suffer. Men, in particular, no longer ruled the world beyond the edge of the forest. Confined to farming and village affairs on the reservation, they were no longer allowed to hunt, fight, or trade beyond the village clearing. Many slid into alcoholism, and the reservations became pockets of poverty in the wilderness.

Before long, the Iroquois tribes abandoned hunting and gathering lifestyles and began to farm the land.

In 1799, Handsome Lake, himself sick and alcoholic, appeared to fall dead. However, he had only lapsed into a coma, during which he had a series of visions. Upon awakening, he declared that he had been taken on a spiritual journey by four messengers. He quit drinking and regained his health. Then, the sixty-four-year-old man began speaking to his people about

Gai'wiio, or the **Good Message**, as he called his new religion. It was a blend of Quaker and traditional Iroquois beliefs. He opposed many white customs, especially the consumption of alcohol, and advocated purification through traditional beliefs. He urged followers to strengthen family and community bonds, share among themselves, and take up farming as a way of life.

Handsome Lake helped his followers adapt to a new world. Today, many Iroquois who call themselves "the Longhouse People" still follow his teachings and repeat his speeches from memory.

Preserving the Mohawk Language

Like Iroquois beliefs, the **Iroquoian language**, too, has continued. Despite being united by a similar overarching language, each of the Iroquois tribes spoke its own dialect. Onondaga was spoken at council, which has given this language great prominence among the Iroquois. Yet Mohawk is one of the languages that is still widely spoken today. For that reason, we have used Mohawk as an example here.

There are a number of ways in which Native American languages may be presented in written English. Two of the more popular books describing the Mohawk language are *One Thousand Useful Mohawk Words* and *Mohawk Language Dictionary*. The following examples are based upon the latter.

The Mohawk language has six vowels pronounced as follows:

> *a* as in *father*
>
> *e* as in *they*, and sometimes as in *met*
>
> *i* as in *see* and sometimes as in *hit*

o as in note

en as in the nasalized "u" of s*u*n

on as in the nasalized "oo" sound in s*oo*n

The Mohawk language consists of eight consonants:

t as in *dog* or as *take* between consonants and at the end of a word

k as in *geese* when before a vowel and as *kite* other times

s as in *sun*, and as in shout when followed by *i* and another vowel

r as in a combined English *r* and *l*. The Mohawk *r* is difficult to pronounce. In some languages, the letter sounds more like an *l*

h as in *hat*, with an aspiration, or puff of air, for emphasis

: This is a glottal stop or pause that doesn't exist in English. It's similar to the *t* in the English "abou*t* *th*ree," when spoken rapidly

Some consonants may be combined as follows:

kh as in *ki*te

kw as in *quiet*, except when preceded by a consonant where the *k* takes on more of a *g* sound

th as in *there*, but with greater emphasis on the *h*

ts as in a combined English *j* and *ch* sound that often occurs before the "i" sound

wh as in father

Accented vowels and syllables are written in capital letters. Here are some examples of everyday words that you might say in the Mohawk language.

akSA:a	boy
rontate:KENwha:	brothers
takos	cat
ekSA:a	child
Onenhste	corn
karhon:	cradleboard
taraktarak	cricket
ohskenONton	deer
rhar	dog
onhwentsia:	earth
rake:NIha:	father
kentsion:	fish
karha:	forest
onkiaTENron	friend
tskwahrhe:	frog
ekSA:a	girl
ki:teRONtaks	home
kanonhsa:	house
watha:	maple
ohNEkari	maple syrup
ihsta	mother
onONta:	mountain
iah	no
ohaha:	path
khe:kEN:a	sister
aROsen	squirrel

These reenactors exchange stories at the Old Fort Niagara State Historical Park in Youngstown, New York.

karahkwa:	sun
ohNEka:	water
HEN:ENhen	yes

Today, Mohawk and other Iroquois languages are being taught on reservations and online. The Mohawk tribe in Brantford, Ontario, for instance, offers a two-year-long language program. It has been teaching classes since 1999, with the goal of creating other teachers as well as capable, confident Mohawk speakers. It is the goal of many Iroquois tribes to inspire younger generations to carry on the traditions, beliefs, and practices of their Native communities.

Today, descendants of the Iroquois tribe include athletes such as Brett Bucktooth, who is a member of the Iroquois National Lacrosse team.

CHAPTER SIX

Man has responsibility, not power.

—Tuscarora Tribe saying

THE NATION'S PRESENCE NOW

The landscape of North America, its population, and its people have changed greatly since the first Iroquois ancestors set foot on North American soil. Since the 1600s, the Iroquois' and other Native American tribes' ways of life have been uprooted. Their once large territories have been reduced to small plots of land, and in many cases, the tribes themselves have been relocated thousands of miles from their ancestral homes. Areas of forest have evolved into cities and towns. Today, some Iroquois have remained on the reservations set aside for them, but more and more, people have left the reservation to pursue a life in urban areas.

Reigniting a Culture

Today, each of the tribes has rekindled its culture, its roots extending from deep in the past to the bustle of modern life. Some ceremonies and beliefs, such as the condolence ceremony, have persisted into the twenty-first century despite hundreds of years of pressure to embrace a Western lifestyle. Many tribes today run hotels and casinos, in addition the daily activities on the reservation.

Over the years, individuals belonging to the Iroquois tribes have become teachers, doctors, engineers, and other professionals. Of special renown are the Mohawk steelworkers, who have been working on girders, high in the sky, constructing bridges and skyscrapers for over one hundred years. Today, out of two thousand union ironworkers employed in New York City, about two hundred are from the Mohawk tribe. The workers, all men, are deeply connected to the profession; some are fourth-generation workers. Most come from reservations in Montreal, Canada, and have a wealth of knowledge that makes them invaluable to the New York City building industry. Their history is one that originated in the 1880s.

In 1883, a group of Mohawks from the St. Regis Reservation found work constructing a bridge at Cornwall, Ontario, in Canada. Other Mohawks worked

Many descendants of the Iroquois tribes have become known for their expert skill as builders of skyscrapers. Here, workers build a skyscraper in New York City in 1964.

on bridges spanning the St. Lawrence River. Their expertise grew, and soon they were working in large US cities such as New York. Men continue to be drawn to this dangerous work, which requires the keen sight, courage, and agility prized by their ancestors. It is believed that these individuals also excel at this work because of their remarkable sense of balance. High steel allows men to work in ways similar to their ancestors. Just as men used to hunt for long stretches, away from their families, so their descendants spend many weeks and months working on projects away from their families. The risky work also offers a prestige similar to that of ancient chiefs.

At mid-century, the populations of reservations had recovered from the lows of 1900, and many families were enjoying some prosperity. Despite state and national policies, the Iroquois have refused to become simply another American minority, though leaders still worry that their heritage will be lost. They are doing all they can to reignite a dedication to the beliefs and traditions of their people. Today, over 100,000 Iroquois live in the United States and Canada. Many live on reservations in New York, although there are three in Canada and others in Wisconsin and Oklahoma.

The longhouses, stone tools, canoes, and buckskin clothes have faded into the past, but many beliefs and customs have endured among the people of the longhouse. At least one longhouse stands in each Iroquois region, no longer as a dwelling but as a center for religious, political, and social activities. The Iroquois have a proud history, which began long before the arrival of the first Europeans, and a culture that flourishes to this day.

Cycle of Ceremonies

The cycle of ceremonies is followed by many people, and the councils continue to meet and make decisions for the Six Nations, according to the Great Law of Peace. The Great Council still meets, and clan mothers appoint sachems, although modern tribal chiefs are now elected. Members of the False Face Society still dance in masks to ensure good health for their people. Artists honor the past through the practice of traditional crafts, and the language of each of the Six Nations is still spoken. Clan mothers still name the children of the clan, and on long winter nights, old men tell stories of the past to the children gathered around them.

Lacrosse is a popular sport with many Iroquois tribes.

The Six Nations Today

Today, the Iroquois are scattered throughout upstate New York, Wisconsin, and Ontario, Canada. Here is a summary of the current status of each of the Six Nations.

The Onondaga Nation

Occupying 7,300 acres (2,954 ha), the Onondaga Nation is located about 5 miles (8 km) south of Syracuse, New York. Around 1,475 people are enrolled, or officially registered, members of the tribe on the reservation. Like their ancestors, the Onondaga still call themselves Haudenosaunee, the "people of the longhouse."

The nation is led by a tribal government of fourteen chiefs and one head chief, selected by the clan mothers. As Keepers of the Council Fire, the Onondaga still host meetings of the Great Council of all Six Nations on the reservation.

On their lands they also have four businesses and a school system. They do not permit drinking of alcohol or allow the building of any casinos or gambling establishments. The tribe is also involved in sports. Onondaga is considered the capital of the Iroquois Confederacy. In 2002, they opened a 1,900-seat, multi-level sports complex, where in 2015, the reservation hosted the annual World Indoor Lacrosse Championships. To learn more about the nation and its activities, visit their website: www.onondaganation.org.

The Oneida Nation

Many Oneidas live on a reservation near Green Bay, Wisconsin. In total, 21,321 members are enrolled in Wisconsin. The Oneida there have a thriving community that offers individuals an opportunity to connect with their ancestors through use of online resources and the Oneida History Program. Members from the Oneida tribe work together to ensure that materials and resources are available for any person wishing to learn more about the Oneida tribe. Part of the website features key information about the tribe, its history, and their actions in the present day. To learn more, visit: www.oneida-nsn.gov.

Over 1,000 people live on a reservation in Oneida, New York. Their 32 acres (13 ha) are all that remain of the 6 million acres (2,428,113 ha) in New York State that once belonged to their ancestors. This traditionalist group was finally recognized by the Bureau of Indian Affairs in 1987, after which a longhouse was built in Oneida territory—the first in over 150 years. In 2015, they opened a twenty-four-hour casino called the Yellow

The Iroquois tribes, such as the Onondaga, hold ceremonies throughout the year.

Brick Road Casino in Chittenango, New York. This facility offered opportunities for the tribe to increase revenue.

Known as the "People of the Standing Stone," the Oneidas acquired their name from the legend that whenever they moved, a stone appeared and gave directions. Until the Oneidas are united, it is said, the stone will no longer guide them. To learn more about the nation, visit: www.oneidaindiannation.com.

The Seneca Nation

As of 2015, the Seneca Nation in New York has a total population of 8,000. Some live on the reservation while others live in villages or nearby cities.

The Seneca Nation is spread over five reservations: the Allegany, the Cattaraugus, the Niagara, the Buffalo, and the Oil Springs Reservations. They are dedicated to making their culture accessible to Native and non-Native people. The nation features a dedicated tourism website, www.senecanation.com, along with their own personal nation website, www.sni.org. Every year, they host lively events, such as powwows, that celebrate Iroquois and Seneca culture.

The Seneca are Keepers of the Western Door, the only Iroquois tribe to own a city—Salamanca, New York. Salamanca is known for being the only city within a reservation in the United States, and for its flourishing hardwoods industry. Maple, oak, and cherry are popular hardwoods in the area.

The Seneca have their own federally recognized government and are a sovereign nation. Their government has executive, judicial, and legislative branches that make decisions for the nation. To help bolster revenue, the Seneca, too, have a casino, the Seneca Allegany Casino, which was established in 2004. They likewise have the Allegany State Park at their doorstep. Because of these businesses, according to the Seneca's website, the Seneca Nation is the "fifth-largest employer in Western New York."

There are three other Seneca settlements in the United States and Canada: the Tonawandas near Akron, Ohio; the Six Nation, or Grand River, Reserve near Brantford, Ontario; and the Seneca-Cayugas, who were relocated to northeastern Oklahoma in the 1800s and still live there.

The Tuscarora Nation

After battling against colonial settlers, some Tuscaroras fled north from their native lands of North and South Carolina in the 1700s to become the sixth nation of the Iroquois Confederacy. In the early part of the eighteenth century, they lived in six towns protected by twelve hundred warriors. Eventually, some returned to their ancestral lands and have worked hard to establish their presence in the area. They have a dedicated website, www.tuscaroranationnc.com, and offer community events such as powwows every year. While the communities in the Carolinas are not federally recognized, they are taking steps to become so.

Today, over 1,150 members of the Tuscarora Nation live on their own reservation in Lewiston, New York. The history of the Tuscarora people stretches past many thousands of years. History remembers them for several instances, but no town remembers them as well as Lewiston. In 2013, the Tuscarora tribe was forever memorialized in its own monument, the Tuscarora Heroes Monument, to commemorate Native Americans saving the lives of Lewiston residents during the War of 1812.

The Mohawk Nation

The Mohawk are traditionally known as the Keepers of the Eastern Door. Today, they reside in reservations throughout Canada and the United States. Altogether, nearly 15,500 people are enrolled in the Mohawk Nation as of 2015.

The St. Regis Mohawk Reservation spans the United States–Canadian border along the St. Lawrence River. Involved with the two countries and three tribal governments of their own, the Mohawks living on this reservation experience one of the most complicated situations of any of the tribes in the Northeast. There is a council on the Canadian side of the reservation,

A building on the St. Regis Mohawk Reservation, circa 2010.

another on the American, and a Tribal Council that oversees all activities.

There is much to see and do on the St. Regis Mohawk Reservation. It houses the Akesasne Mohawk Casino, which provides revenue to the tribe. Likewise, the tribe publishes a monthly newsletter, keeps up-to-date information available via a website, and maintains its own Facebook page, Twitter feed, and YouTube channel. The reservation also has its own school system, health services, and community outreach programs.

Throughout the year, the St. Regis Mohawk Reservation features opportunities to learn traditional Native practices. The Áse Tsí Tewá:ton Experience welcomes people to learn cooking, gardening, and medical techniques, along with hunting and trapping skills and the Mohawk language, Kaníen'keha. To learn more, visit their website: www.srmt-nsn.gov.

The Cayuga Nation

Today, tribal enrollment for the Cayuga Nation is small. In western New York, there are less than 500 people registered. In Oklahoma, nearly 5,060 are enrolled as members. For many decades, the Cayuga Nation has struggled to procure land. As of 2015, they do not have a reservation. However, members of the Cayuga Nation in New York are in talks with New York State to receive an official reservation space.

Despite not having land of their own, the Cayuga Nation of New York does have a dedicated, up-to-date website that details their history, current government, and events. Likewise, the Cayuga Nation owns several businesses in the western New York area. To learn more, visit: www.cayuganation-nsn.gov.

The Seneca-Cayuga Nation in Oklahoma has been a nation since 1832, when the Cayuga living in Sandusky, Ohio, were relocated to what was then known as Indian Territory. Today, the two groups form one nation, joined by their place in the Iroquois Confederacy, and through a shared history that has developed over one hundred years. Their chief, William L. Fisher, periodically communicates with the tribe on their webpage, www.sctribe.com. The website also offers information on news and events.

Continuing the Iroquois

Through the centuries, the Iroquois name has been recounted in many historical texts and firsthand accounts. Today, the members of the once great Confederacy continue their dedication to their tribes and their communities. By teaching the next generation about their ways and beliefs, these nations will ensure their continuance for many centuries more.

The Iroquois chiefs have a proud history. Here, Chief Sunrise poses, circa 1927.

In Iroquois society, leaders are encouraged to remember seven generations in the past and consider seven generations in the future.

—Wilma Mankiller, Cherokee member

FACES OF THE IROQUOIS NATION

Throughout its history, the Iroquois Confederacy has produced many men and women who have made a lasting impression on the tribe and on history in general. These are the names of some of the most well-known tribe members, from older times to the present day.

Louis Deerfoot Bennett (1830–1896), also known as Hottsasodono, meaning "he peeks in the door," was born on the Seneca Nation's Cattaraugus Reservation near Buffalo, New York. As a young man, he was given the name Deerfoot when he outran a horse. After establishing a reputation as a runner in the United States, he traveled to England in search of more track meets and greater prize money. In the early 1860s, he won many long-distance races, usually between 4 and 12 miles (6 and 19 km). With his substantial earnings, he returned to the United States in 1863 and organized a traveling group of runners who entertained audiences around the country. Retiring in 1870, he returned to his home on the Cattaraugus Reservation.

Black Kettle (died 1697) was an Onondaga chief who, as a supporter of the British cause, led his warriors in many battles against the French and their Native American allies. He and his band of warriors raided many settlements and trading posts west of Montreal and also headed attacks on the Algonquins as they attempted to trade with the French. In July 1692, Black Kettle led a group of warriors in an assault on Montreal, escaping with many prisoners. Five years later, he negotiated a peace treaty with the French, but before it was finalized, he was killed by an Algonquin during a hunting trip in what is now western New York.

Beth Brant (1941–), a Mohawk from Ontario, Canada, is a well-known poet, storyteller, editor, and lecturer. She edited *A Gathering of Spirit* (1989), a highly regarded collection of writing and art by Native American women. She has been a lecturer at the University of British Columbia and has made many public appearances. Her work has been included in numerous anthologies and journals. Her own books include *Mohawk Trail* (1985) and *Food & Spirits* (1991).

Joseph Brant (1742–1807), whose Native American name, Thayendanegea, means "he places two bets," was a great Mohawk leader. As a young warrior, he saw considerable action in the French and Indian War (1754–1763) as a British ally. During the American Revolution (1775–1783), he again sided with the British and became a colonel in the British army, fighting alongside General Burgoyne's soldiers. After the war, many Mohawks fled to Canada, and Brant persuaded the king of England to give the Iroquois a land tract in what is now the province of Ontario. Known as Brant County, it is still home to many Mohawk people and other Iroquois descendants.

Molly Brant (circa 1735–1796), the sister of Joseph Brant, married William Johnson, an officer in the British army in a Mohawk ceremony in 1753. When Johnson was knighted for his victory at Lake George in 1755, Molly came to be called Lady Johnson. Serving as hostess at Johnson Hall, she and her husband had eight children.

After her husband's death in 1774, Lady Johnson provided intelligence on American troop movements in the Mohawk valley during the American Revolution. Throughout the war, she continued to be influential among the Iroquois. After the war, she settled in

Ontario, Canada, and was awarded a yearly pension from the British government.

Cornplanter (ca. 1735–1836) was the son of a white trader and a Seneca mother. After his father abandoned him, Cornplanter grew up to become a chief during the French and Indian War, taking part in raids against the British. However, during the American Revolution, he formed an alliance with the British. After the war, he negotiated and signed several treaties with the Americans and often protested the mistreatment of Native Americans.

Cornplanter.

Cornplanter encouraged the adoption of white ways, especially farming practices. In 1796, he received a tract of land in Pennsylvania as a reward for his services. The half brother of Handsome Lake, he received a vision late in life guiding him to end all relations with whites, and he subsequently destroyed all the gifts he had received from officials over the years. In 1960, despite a bitter protest from the Senecas, the Army Corps of Engineers built Kinzua Dam, flooding 10,500 acres (4,249 ha), including Cornplanter's land and his grave.

Hancock (active early 1700s), also known as King Hancock, was a leader in the Tuscarora War of 1711–1713. Originally, the Tuscaroras were friendly toward settlers on their homeland in present-day North Carolina—despite abuses by whites. When Swiss colonists drove Tuscarora families off their land without payment, warriors responded with a series of bloody raids. The Carolina colonies sent in troops, many of them belonging to the Yamasee tribe, to attack Hancock's principal village of Cotechney. The violence continued until 1713 when Tuscarora survivors escaped northward and settled among the five nations of the Iroquois Confederacy. Around 1722, the Tuscaroras formally became the sixth nation in the Confederacy.

Handsome Lake (ca. 1735–1815), half brother of Cornplanter and uncle of Red Jacket, grew up in a traditional Seneca family near present-day Avon, New York. Founder of a new Iroquois religion, he encouraged his people to abandon warfare and learn to farm with horses and plows. Like traditional Iroquois, he received his messages and power from dreams and visions. Handsome Lake was elected to the tribal council in 1801, and he became one of the Seneca leaders to meet with President Thomas Jefferson in Washington, DC. He strongly opposed the loss of Native American lands and the sale of alcohol to his people. In 1850, his beliefs were outlined in the Code of Handsome Lake. As practiced today by followers who still gather in a longhouse, the Longhouse, or Good Message, religion is a blend of Quakerism and Iroquois beliefs. It emphasizes good deeds and silent prayer.

Hendrick (ca. 1680–1755) was Mohican by birth but raised by the Mohawks. In 1710, he was one of four Native Americans, touted as "the four kings of the New World," to visit Queen Anne's court in London, England. When he returned to New York, Hendrick became a spokesperson for the Iroquois Confederacy. A British ally and Protestant convert, he opposed the French but also criticized British failure to defend the frontier. At the battle of Lake George in 1755, he led a band of Mohawk warriors along with British troops under the leadership of William Johnson against the French and their Native American allies. Johnson received knighthood for this great victory, but Hendrick and many of his warriors lost their lives in this battle.

Emily Pauline Johnson (1862–1913), the daughter of a Mohawk chief and an English mother, attended Indian industrial schools through the elementary level. An avid reader, by age twelve she had read many of the literary classics and, as a teenager, she began to have her poems published in literary journals. Her first reading in Toronto, Canada, in 1892 received high praise, and for the next eighteen years she made many public appearances in the United States, Canada, and England. Dressed as a Native American princess, she read her poems and celebrated both her Mohawk and Canadian heritage. Her collections of poetry, including *White Wampum* (1895), *Canadian Born* (1903), and *Flint and Feather* (1913), were very well received. She published a collection of tales, *Legends of Vancouver* (1911), and a novel, *The Shagganappi* (1913).

Oren Lyons in 2007.

Oren R. Lyons (1930–), professor and Native rights advocate, taught American Studies at the State University of New York, Buffalo, for many years. A chief of the Turtle Clan of the Onondaga Nation, he is an artist, editor, and writer. Additionally, he is the publisher of *Daybreak*, a national, Native American news magazine. He has also represented the interests of Native American peoples in the United Nations. "The West didn't get wild until the white people got there," he once said. "There's no such word as 'wild' in the Indian languages. The closest we can get to it is the word 'free'." In 1991, he was the subject of a documentary produced by PBS, *Oren Lyons the Faithkeeper*, and in 2007 he appeared on the show *The Eleventh Hour*, produced by actor Leonardo DiCaprio. Today, he is an advocate for environmental and Native American rights, speaking at colleges and to organizations around the world.

Ely Parker (ca. 1828–1895) studied law but was not allowed to be a lawyer because as a Native American he was not considered a citizen. The grandson of Red Jacket, he collaborated with Lewis Henry Morgan on

the book *League of the Hodenosaunee or Iroquois*
published in 1851. A year later, Parker became chief of
the Seneca and helped the Tonawanda Seneca keep
their reservation. During the Civil War (1861–1865),
he served on the staff of General Ulysses S. Grant and
wrote down the terms of Robert E. Lee's surrender at
the Appomattox Courthouse. When Grant became
president, he appointed Parker to be the first Native
American to become commissioner of Native American
affairs. In this position, Parker worked to maintain
peace with Red Cloud and the Oglala Sioux. "If any
tribe remonstrated against the violation of their natural
and treaty rights, members of the tribe were shot
down and the whole treated as mere dogs," he said.
"Retaliation generally followed, and bloody Indian wars
have been the consequence, costing lives and much
treasure." Fed up with corruption in the United States
government, Parker resigned in 1871.

Maris Bryant Pierce (1811–1874), who was also known
as Hadyanodoh, or Swift Runner, was a Seneca activist
who battled greedy speculators who wanted to trick
Native Americans into selling their land at very low
prices. While still a student at Dartmouth College, he
came to oppose the Treaty of Buffalo Creek of 1838,
which called for the sale of Seneca land to the Ogden
Land Company and removal of the tribe to Indian
Territory in present-day Oklahoma. The tribe lost some
of its land, including the Buffalo Creek reservation, but
was able to retain other reservations because of Pierce's
many efforts. In later years, he became an interpreter
for the Seneca Nation and helped the tribe adopt an

elective system of government. Pierce once stated, "The fact that the whites want our land imposes no obligation on us to sell it, nor does it hold forth an inducement to do so, unless it leads them to offer a price equal in value to us."

A painting of Red Jacket by Seth Eastman, circa 1853.

Red Jacket (ca. 1758– 1830) was an outstanding orator and a great Seneca leader. At the start of the American Revolution, he advocated neutrality but joined the Mohawk, Onondaga, Cayuga, and other Seneca in support of the British. He was named because of the red coat he wore while serving as a dispatch carrier. After the war, he became the principal spokesperson for the Seneca people and sometimes the entire Confederacy. An advocate of traditional customs, he opposed the efforts of missionaries to convert his people to Christianity. Shortly before his death, he said, "I am an aged tree and can stand no longer. My leaves are fallen, my branches are withered, and I am shaken by every breeze. Soon my aged trunk will fall."

Saint Kateri Tekakwitha (1656–1680) was the daughter of a Mohawk chief and an Algonquin captive. When she was only four years old, her parents and baby brother died in a smallpox epidemic. Kateri was left badly scarred but survived the disease. Growing up in a Mohawk village in New York, she became known for her skill and hard work in making wampum.

When she was twenty years old, she was baptized and practiced Catholicism despite persecution from her own people. In 1677, she fled to Canada with a group of Christianized Oneidas. A devout Christian, she hoped to establish a convent, but church authorities rejected her plan. When she died, it is said that a miracle took place—her pockmarks disappeared. In 1884, Kateri became a candidate for canonization. In 1943, she was declared venerable and in 1980, she was declared blessed, which is the second step toward becoming a saint. On October 21, 2012, Blessed Kateri Tekakwitha became Saint Kateri Tekakwitha, an honor in the Catholic Church.

There have been many people who have spoken on behalf of the Iroquois Nation or who have contributed to its survival, and without them, the Iroquois history could have been much different. There were some throughout history who have tried to prevent Native people from keeping their identity. However, many other men and women have committed themselves to continuing the Iroquois legacy, and by doing so they have ensured that many Iroquois traditions, beliefs, and practices continue today.

A stained-glass image of Saint Kateri.

Faces of the Iroquois Nation

CHRONOLOGY

1535 French explorer Jacques Cartier sails up the St. Lawrence River and through Iroquois country.

1570–1600 Hiawatha and Deganawida found the Iroquois Confederacy.

1609 The Dutch discover the Iroquois Nation.

1609–1615 Samuel de Champlain, the governor of New France, helps enemies of the Iroquois attack the Mohawk people.

1640s The Iroquois begin the so-called Beaver Wars against the tribes of the upper Great Lakes.

1662 A smallpox epidemic sweeps through the Iroquois, decimating their population.

1666 The French begin a series of attacks on the Mohawks.

1667 The five tribes of the League agree to a border treaty with the French and their Native American allies.

1672 The Iroquois negotiate a peace treaty with the Algonquins regarding northeastern borders.

1687 The Iroquois conquer the Illinois, Miami, Ottawa, and Hurons.

1689–1763 The Iroquois take part in a series of wars between the English and French, including King William's War (1688–1697), Queen Anne's War (1702–1713), King George's War (1744–1748), and the French and Indian War (1754–1763), collectively known in North America as the French and Indian Wars.

early 1700s The Iroquois Nation attains the peak of its military strength.

1709 The Iroquois break neutrality in Queen Anne's War and aid England.

1713 Queen Anne's War comes to an end.

about 1722 The Tuscarora join as nonvoting members of the League of the Iroquois.

1779 American soldiers attack Iroquois villages during the Revolutionary War.

1784 The Iroquois give up most of their land to the United States in the Treaty of Fort Stanwix.

1794 Signing of the Treaty of Canandaigua.

1800 Seneca leader Handsome Lake establishes the Good Message religion, which is still widely practiced today.

1823 The Oneida begin moving to land near Green Bay, Wisconsin.

1838 The Ogden Land Company takes Seneca land at Buffalo Creek.

1887 The Dawes General Allotment Act encourages assimilation of Native peoples into American society and calls for allotment of reservation lands to individuals.

1900 Populations on reservations drop to the lowest numbers ever and tribal leaders fear that traditional culture will become extinct.

1927 Clinton Rickard, a Tuscarora, organizes the Indian Defense League of America.

1950s Despite Seneca protests, the United States Army Corps of Engineers builds a dam on the Cornplanter Reservation.

1966 Robert L. Bennett, an Oneida, becomes head of the Bureau of Indian Affairs.

1991 Chief Oren R. Lyons is featured in a PBS documentary.

2007 Oren R. Lyons appears in *The Eleventh Hour*, produced by Leonardo DiCaprio.

2012 Kateri Tekakwitha becomes a saint in the Catholic Church.

2015 The Onondaga Nation hosts the World Lacrosse Championships.

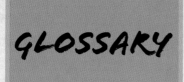

GLOSSARY

Bering Strait The body of water that separates Russia and Alaska. During the last Ice Age, a land bridge across the strait allowed for migration from one continent to the other.

breechcloth A cloth or skin worn between the legs; also called a breechclout.

burden carrier A wooden frame strapped to the back for carrying goods.

clan A number of families related to a common ancestor.

clan mother A respected elder of the longhouse who provided leadership.

cradleboard A wooden board used to carry a baby.

death song A song sung in the midst of battle or right before a Native warrior was about to die.

False Face Society A group of men who wore carved wooden masks, such as "Old Broken-Nose," to frighten the spirits of disease.

gauntlet A form of torture in which two lines of Iroquois warriors would taunt and torment captives as they ran in between them.

Good Message Religion established by Handsome Lake in 1799, now called the New Religion.

Haudenosaunee Iroquoian name for themselves, meaning "people of the longhouse."

hominy Corn kernels without the outer skin.

Irinakhoiw Ojibwa name for the Iroquois, meaning "poisonous snakes."

Iroquoian language A large language group comprising many languages spoken by Native Americans.

Iroquois General names for the Six Nations (Mohawk, Oneida, Onondaga, Cayuga, Seneca, and Tuscarora); pronounced *EAR-ah-koy* in the United States and *EAR-ah-kwah* in Canada.

Iroquois Confederacy The political union of the six Iroquois nations also referred to as the League of the Iroquois.

longhouse A large dwelling covered with elm bark in which several Iroquois families lived.

ohwachira An extended family, including a mother's sisters, brothers, and children, that lived together in a longhouse.

orenda A supernatural force present in all things in nature.

ossuary A place where the bones of the dead are discarded.

reservation An area of land set aside for Native American nations to live.

sachem The Iroquois term for leader or chief.

Sky World An Iroquoian term for the place above the earth where life originated.

sovereignty Having complete control of governmental and other major decisions; supreme power.

succotash A mixture of corn, beans, and hominy that was a staple in the diet of tribes of eastern North America.

three sisters An Iroquoian name for corn, squash, and beans, the three primary and interrelated crops.

Turtle Island The earth (formed on the back of a turtle, according to the Iroquois story of creation); figuratively, North America.

wampum Beads made of white or purple shells; formerly sewn into belts in patterns that symbolized the history of the Iroquois people.

BIBLIOGRAPHY

Berleth, Richard. *Bloody Mohawk: The French and Indian War & American Revolution on New York's Frontier*. Delmar, NY: Black Dome Press, 2009.

Bunson, Matthew, and Margaret Bunson. *Saint Kateri: Lily of the Mohawks*. Seattle, WA: Our Sunday Visitor, 2012.

Cook, Jeanette. *Within a Four Mile Square: The History of the Onondaga Nation*. Bloomington, IN: Xlibris Corp, 2002.

Dunbar-Ortiz, Roxanne. *An Indigenous Peoples' History of the United States*. ReVisioning American History. Boston, MA: Beacon Press, 2015.

Dwyer, Helen, and Amy M. Stone. *Oneida History and Culture*. Native American Library. New York: Gareth Stevens Publishing, 2012.

Hauptman, Laurence M., and L. Gordon McLester III, eds. *The Oneida Indian Journey: From New York to Wisconsin 1784–1860*. Madison, WI: The University of Wisconsin Press, 1999.

Page, Jake. *In the Hands of the Great Spirit: The 20,000-Year History of American Indians*. New York: Free Press, 2004.

Robertson, Robbie. *Hiawatha and the Peacemaker*. New York: Abrams Books for Young Readers, 2015.

Tucker, Toba Pato. *Haudenosaunee: Portraits of the Firekeepers, the Onondaga Nation*. Syracuse, NY: Syracuse University Press, 1999.

Weitzman, David. *Skywalkers: Mohawk Ironworkers Build the City*. New York: Roaring Brook Press, 2010.

White, Louellyn. *Free to Be Mohawk: Indigenous Education at the Akwesasne Freedom School*. Norman, OK: University of Oklahoma Press, 2015.

FURTHER INFORMATION

Want to know more about the Iroquois? Check out these websites, videos, and organizations.

Websites

Iroquois Confederacy and the US Constitution

www.iroquoisdemocracy.pdx.edu

This website explains how the Iroquois Confederacy became a model for the formation of the US Constitution and the US government.

Iroquois Museum

www.iroquoismuseum.org

This website features information about the Iroquois Museum in Howes Cave, New York.

Seneca-Iroquois National Museum

www.senecamuseum.org

This website discusses the Seneca-Iroquois Museum, its exhibits, and the history of the Seneca Nation.

Videos

CrashCourse US History: The Natives and the English

www.youtube.com/watch?v=TTYOQ050DOI

Best-selling author John Green explains the relationship between Native Americans and the first English settlers.

Deganawida and the Great Peace

www.youtube.com/watch?v=3Y9p9iwvlpQ

Learn about the history of Deganawida (here spelled Dekanawida) and the Iroquois Confederacy in this illustrative video.

Oren Lyons's PBS Interview

www.youtube.com/watch?v=i_qj5_PUhlo

The Onondaga Historical Association's YouTube channel features an interview with Chief Oren R. Lyons.

Virtual Tour of Seneca-Iroquois National Museum

www.youtube.com/watch?time_continue=10&v=4FtayT2SX8g

This video gives you a brief tour of some of the exhibits at the Seneca-Iroquois National Museum.

Organizations

Cayuga Nation

PO Box 803

Seneca Falls, NY 13148

(315) 568-0750

www.cayuganation-nsn.gov

Mohawk Council of Kahnawà:ke

PO Box 720

Kahnawà:ke, QC, J0L 1B0

(450) 632-7500

www.kahnawake.com

Oneida Nation of New York

2037 Dreamcatcher Plaza

Oneida, NY 13421

(315) 829-8900

www.oneidaindiannation.com

Oneida Nation of Wisconsin

PO Box 365

Oneida, WI 54155

(920) 869-4921

oneida-nsn.gov

Onondaga Nation

Communications

3951 Route 11

Nedrow, NY 13120

(315) 492-1922

www.onondaganation.org

St. Regis Mohawk Tribe

Community Building

412 State Route 37

Akwesasne, NY 13655

(518) 358-2272

www.srmt-nsn.gov

Seneca-Cayuga Tribe of Oklahoma
23701 S. 655 Rd
Grove, OK 74344
(915) 787-5452
www.sctribe.com

Seneca-Iroquois National Museum
814 Broad Street
Salamanca, NY 14779
(716) 945-1760
www.senecamuseum.org

Seneca Nation
90 Ohiyo Way
Salamanca, NY 14779
(716) 945-1790
www.sni.org

Six Nations of the Grand River
Chiefswood Road
Ohsweken, Ontario N0A 1M0
(519) 445-2201
www.sixnations.ca

Ska-Nah-Doht Iroquoian Village
8348 Longswood Road
Mount Brydges, Ontario N0L 1W0
(519) 264-2420
www.museumsontario.ca/museum/Ska-Nah-Doht-Iroquoian-Village

INDEX

The People and Culture of the Iroquois

The People and Culture of the Iroquois

ABOUT THE AUTHORS

Cassie M. Lawton is a freelance editor and writer living and working in New York City.

Raymond Bial has published more than eighty books—most of them photography books—during his career. His photo-essays for children include *Corn Belt Harvest, Amish Home, Frontier Home, Shaker Home, The Underground Railroad, Portrait of a Farm Family, With Needle and Thread: A Book About Quilts, Mist Over the Mountains: Appalachia and Its People, Cajun Home,* and *Where Lincoln Walked.*

As with his other work, Bial's deep feeling for his subjects is evident in both the text and illustrations. He travels to tribal cultural centers, photographing homes, artifacts, and surroundings and learning firsthand about the national lifeways of these peoples.

The emeritus director of a small college library in the Midwest, he lives with his wife and three children in Urbana, Illinois.